I HEAR THE MUSIC ~ I HAVE TO GO

BY FRANK M. PAWLAK

My story of bringing music, humor, and encouragement to those in Assisted Living Facilities and Rest Homes for more than 50 years

Order this book online at www.trafford.com
or email orders@trafford.com

Most Trafford titles are also available at major online book retailers.

Printed in the United States of America.

ISBN: 978-1-4269-5923-3 (sc)
ISBN: 978-1-4269-5924-0 (hc)
ISBN: 978-1-4269-5925-7 (e)

Cover design by Annie Trout

Library of Congress Control Number: 2011903897

Trafford rev. 08/31/2011

 www.trafford.com

North America & international
toll-free: 1 888 232 4444 (USA & Canada)
phone: 250 383 6864 ♦ fax: 812 355 4082

INDEX

FORWARD

If you don't know what to do with your life, find out what someone else needs you to do for him or her, and do that.

Although the author of this book is my eldest brother and twelve years my senior, no subject could be more pertinent to that vast assembly known among sociological labelers than us "Baby Boomers". The time is quickly approaching that we are rolling down the physical, economical and employable hill like the proverbial "snowball headed for...who knows what!"

Frank Pawlak has projected upon the huge, high definition screen of comprehension images of inevitability awaiting us all. Not since Noah survived "The Deluge" and the "Divine" declared, "The day of man shall be three score and ten" (70 years), have people lived as long as they are living today.

As you are taken on this journey of the author's most powerful memories, you will be invited to enter the secret attic of the sacred past. You will see the aged as antique footlockers full of treasures yet to be discovered. You will find someone who needs you to do something for them and you will do just that.

Like many who will read this book, I recalled memories of my own father. My Dad loved golf, but with time his flexibility lessened and his drives off the tee shortened. However, one day he drove one farther that I had ever seen him hit a golf ball. He quickly announced, "Yes sir boys, once there was an Arnold Palmer in this old body."

As Frank Pawlak walks us down the hallways of the Assisted Living Facilities and Nursing Homes, we see the frail little lady in the wheelchair that once had a Raquel Welch in that old body. As we are guided into the Dining Hall and we see the shaking hands try to negotiate the soup to the mouth without a spill, we are reminded of the hands that once wrestled that steering wheel through the number one turn at the Friday Night Speedway. As the slipper shod feet shuffle a few inches at a time behind the metal walker, the author helps us see the feet that left that gymnasium floor to snatch down the rebound and start the fast break that would win the "State Championship". More sobering are the confused eyes and weak voice that ask their own child, "Do I know you?" This is the same mind that once created a plan that produced millions of dollars for that Fortune 500 Corporation.

If you ever held a sleeping baby close to your breast or danced across a Ball Room floor with beautiful women in your arms, or rubbed that little round head and ruffled the hair of a laughing child, or lifted that wedding veil and kissed the most precious lips under Heaven; then this book has a glaring question. At what age do we no longer require touches, pats, hugs, or kisses?

As I have laughed and cried my way through this book I must give you a warning. Unless you want to touch a life, unless you want to become a better person than you are, or unless you want to hope someone will be there for you in your twilight years, DON'T READ THIS BOOK. If you read this book I am confident you will find an elderly person near you and visit them, read to them, sing to them, hold their hand, touch them and experience what it does for you.

Samuel P Pawlak, Sr.

DEDICATION

Thanks to the love of my life, my wife Leigh Ann.
My soul mate & scribe.
The Dictionary say's a scribe is someone that writes or
copies words.
I wrote and she somehow deciphered my missed
spelled words and copied them.
This book would have been impossible without wthe
late nights of her devotion.

CHAPTER ONE

THE OLD COOLSPING PLACE

First time I saw it I thought it was the biggest
red brick house I'd ever seen. My brother and I
had just walked about a mile or so through the
old Polish neighborhood. We stopped to watch a
man with a push cart going from house to house
ringing a bell and people would come out and
bring their knives and scissors to be sharpened
by hand; but we rushed on to see the big house
where Mom and Dad said we were moving.

It was the fall of '44 and the war was going strong. Our imaginations were as big as the war itself. By the next year we were marching all over the fields and high grass, then crawling into the Plum Orchard to fight Hitler, Mussolini, and Tojo; as well as shooting snipers out of the Apples Trees. We were trying to do our part to bring home our Uncles and all the men from our church and town. However, on the day we first saw the place with weeds growing up over the downstairs windows; we could have never known that this old house would be the place in which everything that was going to happen to us was going to take place there.

We just called it the Old Coolspring Place. A big two story with basement and attic; built sometime during the Depression by some Chicago guys that will remain nameless. From time to time a man would come to work on the old house when the "heat" was on in Chicago. He told us boys to just call him "Uncle Pete". A couple of times a year his big black Packard would pull up to the house; out stepped Uncle Pete with a great big smile. He would then bow and say, "Yours Truly". He seemed like such a nice man ~ like Santa Claus. There was, though, another life Uncle Pete had that boy's our age knew nothing about until years later.

A year after we moved in, our Grandmother and Aunt moved into the downstairs quarters. Whenever Uncle Pete was around trying to fix one thing or another; he would knock on my Grandmother's door. When she opened it he would bow and say, "Yours Truly". Then he would ask to borrow a hammer, or screwdriver, or something he never seemed to have in his tool box. After my Grandmother or Aunt gave him the proper tool, they would close the door, laugh and ask, "Why in the world doesn't he say thank you or something else?" He always said, "Yours Truly".

As I look back on those days of Uncle Pete, I realized proper language skills were not his strong point, not for the business he was in. Stories came out later of police chases, and hideouts. To this day the stories get bigger each time they're told. Somehow I think if Uncle Pete were here today and could hear those stories or were asked about them; I believe he would just bow and say, "Yours Truly".

In the 40's and 50's is where it all began in the Old Coolspring Place.

One day when I was about 9 years old, I was playing with some old toy while lying down on the floor of our upstairs flat. My Dad was playing the guitar and singing some old Western song, "Just Riding Down the Canyon". Dad strummed a minor cord (I think now it may have been an E minor), and I jumped to my feet and said, "Teach me how to play that Dad!!" Well that day, needless to say, was when my guitar playing started. I eagerly began to practice day after day, hour after hour. Soon I began to play in church. The only two cords I knew were C&G, but I was up there playing. The piano and other instruments drowned me out so that only the real musicians would know I played the same cords over and over from "When the Roll Is Called Up Yonder" to "The Lord's Prayer", each number got equal time. As I practiced at home up in the attic; I'd strum and sing with all my heart. Then one day something happened that would start me on a course for over 50 years now.

Mr. Mac came to me after church one night and asked, "Son, why don't you go with me next Thursday evening to the Rest Home?" (That's what they were called back then.) Mr. Mac told me that Rest Homes were where I could play and sing, and then he would tell them what was studied in Sunday School class last week. He told me they will love it.

The following Thursday evening at 7:00 I was ready and waiting when Mr. Mac pulled up in front of the house. I carefully placed my guitar in the back seat and away we went. I kept thinking of his words, they rolled over and over in my mind; "Just sing and play for them son, they will love it."

Today after all those years, as my wife and I pull up in front of an Assisted Living Facility, or Nursing Home I can still hear Mr. Mac's words. So now I turn to my wife and say, "Honey they are going to love it when you sing for them." Oh, by the way they always do. We have met some of the most wonderful people in our travels, and as we drive away we'll look at each other and say that they had done so much more for us than we had for them.

Mr. Mac always reminded me of Abe Lincoln; a tall, rawboned man. One of the last times we talked he told me again about all the years he went to the Pacific Garden Missions in Chicago. This is where Billy Sunday had become a Christian; quit his Baseball career with the Cubs to become a great Evangelist. Billy would say, "God don't just save to the utter most, but He saves to the **gutter** most!!"

Mr. Mac had happy times in recalling his years in mission work; but he had plenty of heartaches too. I remember one evening he was driving through one of the South Chicago neighborhoods, and saw some boys playing ball. The ball rolled into the street and one boy ran after it. He fell down just as Mr. Mac was driving by. The boy was run over by a back wheel and killed. I don't believe Mr. Mac ever got over that; he loved children so much.

Nevertheless, he went week after week to the mission. He told me that if he could have his way when he died it would be with his arm

around one of those men at the Mission he was telling about Christ. Only in heaven will we know just how many lives were changed from the Rest Home to the mission in Chicago. That baton was passed on to me years ago; my wife and I have been in this ministry together for quite some time now, and there is still so much more to do.

Life can seem so strange sometimes, after all the years that Mr. Mac worked with those folks in the Nursing Homes, etc..., he developed Alzheimer's. However, he never lost the love of going to church. Often on his way home he would become confused; people would find him on the main street in town, and because everyone knew him they would stop, talk to him and have him follow them back to his house. Maybe the disease was a blessing some way, because when his only son died he really didn't know what happened. Then when his Grandson was hit by a speeding car and killed he was saved from that awful pain because the Alzheimer's had progressed quite severely. I believe had he known it would have brought back those heartbreaking memories of that night in South Chicago and the pain of that family who had lost their little boy under the wheels of his car.

When I received the news that Rev. Mac had gone to his reward, I was living in Florida. I was unable to make the trip back North for his funeral; but my mind went back to all the things I saw and learned from him in those Rest Homes; and somehow I knew Mr. Mac was smiling down on me. As I got my old guitar out, I could almost hear him say again, "Go on to the next place if you will, sing and play for those people son. They will love it."

CHAPTER TWO

THE PRIDE OF FLAG AND COUNTRY

It was at the Old Coolspring Place where we heard the good news that World War II had ended. My brother and I wanted to join in with all the church bells that were ringing, the factory whistles blowing, and the few neighbors who had cars and were blowing their horns. So we took the only things we had which were long stick matches to celebrate. We held them in a pair of pliers and hit them on the concrete steps of the front porch and then we laid some of them down flat and hit the red & white lighting ends to make them sound like caps going off. Yes, oh yes, we were celebrating that the war was over.

I remember the fruit basket Uncle John brought by the house before he went off to war. Now he and our other Uncles were coming home. I still have those V~mail letters that I received from the war zone; but they couldn't say in the letter where they were, or what was going on. My Uncle said he thought he was in North Africa at that time, but he wasn't really sure.

I can still remember the smell of sulfur that burned as those long stick matches made their popping and crackling sounds. We thought that day was the end of all wars; but as I am writing this book I have just said goodbye to a young man I met 6 months ago as he is on his way to Iraq; leaving behind his wife and two small sons, the baby just turned 2 years old. **MY GOD, I HATE WAR!**

Some of the people in the Nursing Homes, and Assisted Living Facilities have their memories of war also. When we sing the service songs such as, "Anchor's Away", "As The Army Goes Rolling Along", "From The Halls Of Montezuma To The Shores Of Tripoli", "Off We Go Into The Wild Blue Yonder", or "Grand Old Flag". These heartfelt Americans wave the little flags we pass out to them. Oh my how they wave those flags as they sing along with us. We see the tears run down those old cracked and wrinkled faces. Once again remembering their comrades that never made it back home from Normandy to New Guinea, some lost at Pearl Harbor or The Battle of the Bulge. They'll take their old withered hand that once carried a gun in battle to wipe away a tear. They must have thought from time to time there couldn't be any tears left.

When we ask them to say the Pledge of Allegiance with us, I have seen them struggle to get up from their wheel-chairs to put their hand over their heart as they try to balance themselves with the other hand to keep from falling. At that time my wife and I try to fight back our tears; after all we are trying to lead them.

When we get ready to go down the road to the next place they hold our hands, pat our face, and beg us to please not forget them and to come back. They always say that this is what they need so much more of. Why don't you come more often? **PLEASE!!!**"

Never could I have imagined on that August day in 1945 that in a few years I would be playing and singing for some of those people that were coming home from the war. That each Thursday evening would be a new story, and that I would meet someone else that would become a new friend.

I remember one New Year's Eve up in the old attic; I was listening to the radio I had just gotten for Christmas. I always loved sports and they were broadcasting the Tangerine Bowl's big football game. I didn't know where that was, but it sure sounded nice. I found out later it was in Orlando, Florida. It is now called the Citrus Bowl. There is a baseball field next to the stadium where our youngest son had his try outs for the Minnesota Twins. How could I have ever imagined on that cold January night I would one day walk across that field, sit in the dugout drinking water out of the same fountain so many superstars had drank form. You know I still wish they called it the Tangerine Bowl.

Somehow on a cold snowy winter night the thought of Tangerines makes me feel a little warmer. After the game, I got my old guitar out and tuned it up for Thursday night; to once again sing and play as the New Year came in January 1, 1950.

HOW MY POLISH ROOTS BROUGHT HOPE & JOY

That first old people home smelled so bad when you first went in. I guess they got use to it, but I'm not sure how anyone could. I was told they had goats downstairs under the place. I never saw them, but I never doubted the story either. I believe from that first time as a young man, I saw things that let me know no matter how bad things were in my life there was always someone else who had it worse.

I saw what music did to help them forget some of their sadness for at least an hour or so every

Thursday night. I heard of a sign in front of a church that read, "They that sing, pray twice." We feel we are leading the folks in prayer each time they sing along with us. I have said for years, "Music is like a cup of coffee, it's always better when it is shared with someone else."

I remember a few weeks had gone by for our Thursday night music, when one of the directors informed me that many of the residents were unable to come out of their rooms to see me and be a part of the singing. I replied by asking if it would be possible to go to their rooms and sing for them there. She smiled with great joy and said, "Absolutely!" So as she took me back to little half lit rooms, I began to go from one to another. Then I came to a room where one little old lady was lying in a bed that looked much too large for her small frame. I would say she was probably a larger woman when she was younger, but in the dim lights of the room she looked more like a small child.

The nurse said, "This is Marie, but we have a problem for no one can really talk to her because she doesn't speak a word of English. She only speaks Polish. We only know a few words." Well I felt my heart jump in my chest and informed the nurse that I was Polish, and my family came here from Poland. I then went to the director and asked if I could bring my Dad the following week to talk to Marie while I played and sang for the others, and of course I could.

I couldn't wait for that week to go by. Dad agreed to come with Mr. Mac and myself that next week. When we walked into Marie's room, Dad began speaking right away in Polish by asking her how she was doing. That little woman sat straight up in bed and began to cry as she grabbed for my father's hand. She started talking, begging for Dad not to leave her for there was so much she had to say.

Marie had been there for several years, but no one could talk to her, really talk. No one knew just when she had come to live there. She had no family or friends, I believe she lost everyone. Somehow she was brought to this country after losing them in the Holocaust.

Dad tried to calm her down as he asked to make a deal with her. He told her that if she would let him go on that night, he would bring his brother along the following week who spoke better Polish than he did. Uncle John was always at my Great Grandparent's house next door, and Great Grandma only spoke Polish. As a matter of fact, I remember when Uncle John had gone off to war, Great Grandma had a stroke. She had no feeling in her legs or feet. Dad and Mom took me with them to visit her, which turned out to be the last time before she died. I recall being barely able to look up over the side of the bed to see her. She didn't know anyone. The family discussed if Uncle John was there if she would have known him.

So when I saw Marie, it reminded me of my Great Grandmother; who had come on a big boat years ago. She had landed in Baltimore, Maryland then came to the Chicago land area. Dad told Marie that he and his brother would be there the next Thursday evening, and sure enough they were there. Each Thursday evening while Mr. Mac and I had a little service up in the front room; Dad and Uncle John went back to Marie's room. They talked and talked about her times in the old country, as well as stories that the three of them only knew. I wish I could have heard those stories myself; but the music was calling me to the big front room for another service. Marie's story was one of the first of many I would see over the next 50 years.

CHATPER THREE

AFTER ALL THESE YEARS, GOD STILL LOVES AND CARES

THE AMAZING POWER OF BAPTISM

The winter of 1956 seemed colder than usual. I had a Pastor friend ask me if I would go with him to visit two women who wanted to know if there was any way possible to baptize their Mother in the bathtub. You see, she was in her

90's and quite frail. My friend and I agreed we knew of no reason why we couldn't. Her daughters brought out a bathing cap for her dainty head. They got towels, blankets, and the old coal stove as hot as possible. Then the two of us took her by each little frail arm (now only skin and bones) and gently placed her into the tub. We baptized that little lady right there in her bathtub, then brought her carefully out again so her daughters could tend to her. Drying her off and then covering her with a large warm blanket, they laid her in the living room on the sofa in front of that roaring hot stove where she drifted off to sleep. My friend and I left the comforts of that little house and walked across the yard with the snow crunching under our feet. We smiled and agreed that this was a first.

The next morning one of the daughters called and informed us that her mother had passed away in the night. They both thought their mother just couldn't be at peace until she had been baptized and thought she went off to sleep so then later she could go serenely to heaven.

THE BIG QUESTION

While making visitation rounds one day in the hospital, I saw an elderly woman sitting in a chair with a bag of belongings in her hand and some by her feet. I introduced myself as one of the local pastors, and asked, "Are you getting ready to go home, and waiting for your family to pick you up?" She answered, "No. I have no place to go." Then through tears she said, "Pastor, I've lived for the Lord all my life. I have no family, no home, no place to go. I sure hope God knows what He's doing this time." When I tell this story at Nursing Homes and Assisted Living Facilities, I see so many mothers, fathers, grandparents shaking their heads as if to say, "Yes! That's how I feel sometimes."

I talked to a man in Florida a few years ago, and got around to telling him about my wife and I working in these facilities. He told me that his mother was living in one herself. I asked how she was doing; he replied that he didn't know because after he had dropped her off 14 years before, he had not heard from her since. Frustrated and shocked I said, "You haven't heard from her?!! How about her hearing from you?!!" Sad to say, these kinds of stories happen more often that we realize.

A HOUSE VS. A HOME

Out of the many funerals I have conducted there is one in which I told a story I cannot forget. There was a little girl that came to school one day; her family had come to town looking for work. Her clothes were tattered and worn. The teacher questioned her about the situation. The little girl replied, "My Mother, Father, and I are living in our car until my Daddy finds work." This went on for a few weeks; each morning the little girl would show up ready for class. Finally one day the teacher said, "Oh honey, I will be so glad when you and your parents get a home." The little girl looked up at her and with a big smile simply said, "We have a home. We just don't have a house to put it in yet." We see so many people in these facilities that miss their home. They tell us so frequently, "I lost my home." They never say, "My house."

I believe if only people could see the look on some of these Senior's faces when we visit their rooms, and they show us little gifts their children and/or grandchildren had given to them. They just light up and smile as they brag on them and show us their pictures. It's not the value of the gift but just to know their family loves and cares for them.

Then we have seen the ones with the sad faces; like the one little lady who asked me if I knew where a certain small town was. I did and it made her so happy for this was her hometown. She asked when my wife and I leave and drive past the place, if we would stop and tell the people there where she was. She just knew they were wondering about her and where she was; for it had been such a long time since they had seen each other.

I have had people say to me, "I have no talent." "I can't play and sing." etc…. Well my answer to those people is perhaps you are not able to do those things, but you can go and volunteer to stop by one day a week and just sit down and talk to these wonderful people, or better yet, **listen** to them!

Here is an example. A man told me that he and his wife take their Golden Retriever each week to the Nursing Home. The people just love to pet and talk to that dog. Somehow this amazing animal knows where they are going each week when his wife asks, "Are you ready?" Their Retriever begins to jump and whirl around with excitement. They all get into the car and away they go to bring joy to so many. **So if you don't have talent, give your dog a chance and take them to these wonderful people.** As

I've mentioned before in an earlier chapter, one wonders who got more reward out of it them, you, or the dog. I wish I could get people as excited to go to those places as that Golden Retriever. Maybe it has something to do with the fact that he was saved from being put to sleep at the pound. If he really knows where he is going, he just might remember how lonely one can be when you are by yourself.

CHAPTER FOUR

PEOPLE AND FACES WE'LL NEVER FORGET

After my wife and I had been doing this work for a long time, we were booking more and more places to go every day. At one time we had gotten ourselves booked into about 50 facilities per month. I thought maybe I could get some businessmen I knew to help underwrite our work since we had a lot of traveling now. Because of being in the furniture business for years, there was one businessman in particular I went to see.

He was one of the wealthiest men in town. I told him of our need to do more and more of the Assisted Living Facilities and Nursing Homes. He said, "Man, you and your wife need help. This is a great work!! Let me talk to my board of directors. Get back with me in a couple of weeks; but you and your wife have to have some help." Well I was so excited that morning two weeks later. I walked into his office and his secretary buzzed him to let him know I was there.

When I went in, he just said they were not going to do anything. I couldn't speak. All I could do was look at him; the blood must have run out of my face. He said, "The board and I agreed. There is nothing in it for us." I seemed to hear that phrase over and over for a long time when I would think about him and his words ~ "There's nothing in it for us."

There was one place we sang; in fact my wife and I were asked to be Chaplains for that Nursing Home where I knew one of his family members lived. I told him, "Well maybe someday you will be in a place like that and we'll sing for you." He snidely remarked, "I HOPE SO!!"

Today this man is very ill with Parkinson's disease. I wonder if he ever thinks about those words that day. (<u>WHAT'S IN IT FOR ME?!!</u> <u>THERE'S NOTHING IN IT FOR US!!</u>)

<u>WELL THIS IS WHAT'S IN IT FOR US</u>

A short time ago while working in a furniture warehouse; I saw what had been a beautiful new table. However, something had gone terribly wrong. Either it had been dropped off the dock, or one of the many lift trucks racing back and forth loading the trucks ran into it. Looking closer, I saw the scrolled trim that was broken away from the facing, and a door that now hung by one lonely hinge; the high gloss finish was now full of cracks, almost like a piece of ice that had been shattered. Now it sits by itself off to one side never to be used for what it was made for in the mind of the designer: never to be the pride and joy of some family never to be passed down from generation to generation as a family heirloom. I thought how like some people we have met in our travels, and through our ministry; they also feel they have never reached the potential that their Creator had in mind for them. So once again we try to pick up the pieces and see if something can be mended while there is still hope.

I know some that will be reading this book are those that are always trying to fix something, sometimes a life that seemed as destroyed as that table on the dock. Those that are always and forever trying to fix a relationship, to help a child whose "gone wrong", or maybe a ministry that just can't get all the broken pieces back in place: but for all of us ~ where there is life, there is hope. So you see it's not splintered wood, or a beautiful shiny finish, but crushed hearts, and too many disappointments to count, but we will try again. We will sing another song, lead them in the
Lord's Prayer, and tell them that "Jesus loves you".

Here are some of those stories.

A HURTING SOUL

In Tampa there was a woman sitting on a bench waiting for a bus. We had stopped for a red light and my wife looked to her right and saw what she described as the saddest face she had ever seen. Right then the light changed and we had to get out of the way of traffic. My wife yelled, "STOP THE CAR!!!!!!!" I couldn't, but she told me that the woman had locked eyes with her and she felt she heard that woman's soul cry out "HELP ME!" This woman seemed to be so beaten down and didn't want to face one more day of hell. That is what my wife saw. Someone living a life of hell, my wife just wanted to tell her that God knew her need and that Jesus does love her and that there was help and hope. She never got that chance and grieves for this hurting soul. To this very day my wife prays for this woman and can't get that image out of her mind.

BATTERED AND LOST

Another time and place we had stopped for lunch when a poor young lady had walked in sobbing. Her eyes were blackened, clothes torn; asked the manager shyly if there was any chicken that was going to be thrown out, and if she could have a little to feed her children. The manager said that as much as she would like to help it was against policy and turned her away. Humiliated, she ran out so fast that even though we tried to find her to tell her we would buy food for her and the children; she was gone. Unable to be found, all we knew to do then was pray for her.

Odd but true, it seems that there are just some situations beyond our control to help in what we think is helping, yet what we seem to think is the lest we can do, is probably in the scope of eternity the most important~**Prayer**.

These memories have happened on the road traveling. This next person we met was in one of our services.

WENT IN A WIFE ~ CAME OUT A WIDOW

There are people that just seem to get your attention when we are singing and playing. A woman in one of the Assisted Living Facilities caught our attention because she just sat there; never making any motion one way or the other. After we were through she came up to us and shared her story. Just about two weeks before she and her husband had gone out to dinner. He had excused himself to go to the restroom. He opened a door which he thought led to the Men's Room, fell down a flight of stairs and broke his neck. The unmarked, unlocked door was to the basement. The only thing this woman knew was that she was a widow; her children had no room or time for her and that she was in an unfamiliar place left all alone to try to figure out not only what happened to her, but what would she do.

Just imagine yourself one minute a happy woman (man), then next a devastated widow (widower). Someone has to help these poor hurting people.

CHAPTER FIVE

NEVER GIVE UP

I was fifteen years old, standing at the front window of the Old Coolspring Place looking to the North. I saw a storm coming in over Lake Michigan. The clouds were so dark and black that it seemed scary as I looked into them. Then I saw a church steeple. Jetting into the sky was a golden cross on top of the steeple. Watching the clouds grow darker as they rolled in, the cross was growing brighter. That sight, that stormy day lead me to write a song in which I appropriately titled, "The Golden Cross". That storm and cross are just like our lives. The main line in the song says, "The darker that the clouds will roll the brighter that the cross will glow to prove His love He has for you and me." This later grew into the name of our Ministry and Television Program ~ Golden Cross Ministries.

During this time of my life is when I began to learn the upholstery trade. There was an old upholstering shop on the South side of town on the main street. Walking past the shop one day I saw a chair sitting in the window on display. Fascinated by the way the inside back was made; I stopped to take a closer look at the chair. It had long channels running vertically and the way the fabric was tufted in each channel it was just beautiful. All I could do at that moment was just stand there and stare at that chair. Then I decided to go inside to see if they needed any help. There was a large man that spoke to me by asking, "Can I help you kid?" Looking around at all the beautiful sofas, chairs, ottomans, and antiques I blurted out, "Yes sir. Do you need any help?" He smiled at the other upholsterers working on the horses and benches and asked, "What can you do?" "I'll do anything sir. I have an Uncle who is an upholsterer." I thought that would qualify me for a foot in the door. Next I mentioned the shop where he worked. He then replied as he stretched his 6' frame another 2-3 inches, "Oh ya, those fellows are pretty good upholsterers, but not like we are in a custom shop." I found out first hand that day what pride real craftsman took in their work before they signed their signature to any piece they had done.

Well he asked me when I could start working, and I told him right then. So he told me to follow him to the back of the shop where they stripped the furniture. This shop refinished a lot of furniture. The next thing I knew I was putting on the rubber apron, rubber gloves, big rubber boots, and goggles he gave me. Then he showed me how to use the paint and varnish remover with a brush and scraper, and showed me how to prep the frames for refinishing. As he walked away to answer one of the upholsterers questions; he must have laughed at the way I looked with all that garb on. I thought how can I walk across the room without falling down or try to hold up this apron, and with those over sized goggles I must have looked like a W.W. I pilot in a double winged airplane.

That was the beginning of my upholstery career. God knew way back then that I would have to make outside income from time to time to do the ministry in which he was preparing me to do. There were churches I pastored in which I received a salary, but somehow I was always involved in the furniture business. I like to think I am a bit like the Apostle Paul. He was a tent maker and even when the people called for him to come and pray for the sick; he gave them a piece of his shirt or canvas he was working on to take to the sick person and they were healed. Today we call this a prayer cloth. I am quite sure that Paul would have loved to go pray for them himself, but I have always said he had orders to get out. So for some reason or another, I have had to work most of my ministry.

I moved on from the first shop to another. One day a large upholstery company about twelve miles away needed upholsterers. I went to the factory and had an interview with the personnel manager. (I had been his paperboy years ago.

Each Saturday I would collect the fifteen cents due for each week's paper delivery.) I told him where I had been working, and that I was with my Uncle. He thought that was great and knew that they were good guys as well as good upholsterers. "We are in need of some good upholsterers." he told me; and with that I was there the next morning at 7:30 sharp ready to start work.

I had never worked on the kind of large over stuffed furniture that was coming down the assembly line straight at me. It was what they called a 4 man line. One put in the seat, another the arm (there were two of those, one for each side), another for the inside back (which the arm guys helped). It was a moving line where the platform was hooked to a reel assembly line. You were expected to move right along with the piece of furniture and it had to be done by the time it reached the end; or the line would have to shut down. I didn't know what in the world I had gotten myself into, but God knew. He sent a man to help me. He worked on the line for a few years; he knew the job well. About 10 am I said, "Jack, I don't think I can do this. I'm holding you three guys back. I've never seen this kind of upholstery before." He said, "Just stay with it. You know all the basics, and I will help you." He is one man I will never forget. I stayed long enough with that company to become his foreman. We both had a few laughs about that. It didn't happen fast though; it took some years to get there.

There was another man that worked there I remember. The first time I saw him work he was putting in a diamond back. Just the way he made his cuts and pulls as he worked on that piece of furniture was pure beauty and art. This was long before I became a foreman. He also worked with me, showing me some of his techniques. He just seemed to be so unhappy with life. It was just the look on his face. One day while we were working together, I was trying to make what seemed to me a difficult cut and pull. He cursed and swore and told me there are some guys that will never be an upholsterer and you are one of them. I felt so many times that I was so inadequate. Sometimes my hands would literally shake, but I continued to try, try, and try. At sometime it did become easier. I had a chance to leave the factory and open my own little shop. My mother said, "If you will just go into your own business, you'll do well." I did just that. Let me tell you there are a million stories from those days.

I believe the most memorable is the day a small lady came to the shop and introduced herself as Joe's wife. This was the fellow that told me I would never be an upholsterer. She asked me if I knew that Joe had died. I said that I did, and that I believed I had seen it in the paper. She went on to tell me that Joe had always done side work at home. Just before his passing he had taken in a big job from the City (I guess he knew some of the Board members). She said that she had all the materials, etc…, but had no one to finish the job, and asked me if I would be willing to help her do it. I said that I would be glad to in between my jobs. She never knew the cruel things Joe had said to me about never making it as an upholsterer, and I never told her. When I had finished the job, she was so thankful. I have often thought that it was really something that the one man who told me I would never make it; ends up being the one who finished his last job he ever had on this earth.

Over and over we get the chance to do the last thing for someone; sing a song, read a scripture, look into their old tired eyes and tell them one last time that God loves them, and that the next time they hear it they well be hearing from Jesus Christ Himself! So if you have had a Joe in your life that has told you you'll never be a _____ (fill in the blank). **<u>Don't believe it!</u>** God is just preparing you to finish the job!!

CHAPTER SIX

FOR I KNOW THE PLANS I HAVE FOR YOU...

JEREMIAH 29:111

In the Bible we find many promises of encouragement. One of my favorites is Jeremiah 29:11 "For I know the plans I have for you," declares the Lord, "plans to prosper you and not to harm you, plans to give you hope and a future."(NIV)

We have lived in Florida from time to time. During the late 1980's I once again had a successful upholstery shop. All the years of ministry were helped by the business. So often we received no pay for the things we felt we had been called to do.

I met a man through a decorator who worked for me; she told me his name was John and that he was a great upholsterer, but he was deaf and it would be difficult to communicate with him. He was a great guy and he did come to work for me.

John and I became very close. We would write notes to each other, and then he started to teach me a few signs. My youngest son was also working with us. He too began to learn some signs. I realized that I would love to be able to communicate better. I was quite slow at it. Someone had told me of a signing class at the local college. Excited about the idea of learning more, I enrolled 3 nights a week; between work and classes it was quite a load. I studied as hard as I could. Two of my teachers knew John because the deaf community is closely knit.

After a few weeks went by, one of the teachers would ask me for a specific sign. I would use one of the signs John taught me and they would stop me and say, "Wait, wait you didn't learn that in class, we haven't gotten that far yet." We would then laugh because they knew John had been teaching me short cuts. I had the book "The Joy of Signing". I still use it to this day.

My son and I would go over what I was learning in school and he seemed to pick it up fast. He lived next door to me. Early one morning he rang the door bell. I was still in bed, but got up and answered the door. There stood my son; I couldn't figure out what was wrong. His neck was swollen 3-4 times its normal size. It looked like his head and neck were all one size. He could hardly speak. He had been water skiing in the Indian River and got some kind of infection. I told him that I would take him to the doctor at once. I drove as fast as I could. We walked in and when the nurse saw him she ran to the back and immediately got the doctor. He took one look and said to get my son to the hospital as quickly as possible and that he would call ahead and have them waiting for him. Speeding back down Highway 1, we got to the hospital. However, when we got inside he couldn't open his mouth; he was just barely able to crack his lips. They began to ask him questions, "How did it happen?", "Where were you?" on and on. The only way he could answer was to sign to me and then I could tell the nurses. The head nurse told me that just the week before another person had come in who could not hear or speak and what a help I would have been then. They rushed my son right back to one of the rooms and promptly gave him I.V.'s and medication. They came and informed me that he needed to rest and that the oxygen was helping him breath. Relieved, I decided to go get something to eat. As I did, something inside me made me think I should run back to the hospital to make sure he was alright.

As I walked up the long hallway toward his room, I saw three people running with someone on a gurney. They were running so fast that as they past me I couldn't even recognize that it was my son. They had to perform an emergency tracheotomy to save his life. The doctor told me later another two minutes and he wouldn't have made it. He was in I.C.U. for about two weeks. He had lost a lot of weight; after that he returned a few times to the hospital for additional treatments.

One day it dawned on me, that I went to signing school trying to help another man's son so that I could communicate better with him: yet through signing, my son and I were able to get him admitted fast which then, when needed, gave the doctors the extra time necessary to save his life. Today I think of the business man I mentioned in an earlier chapter who had refused to help me, his words ring in my ears again, "There's nothing in it for us." The day I enrolled in that signing class wasn't for me; I did it to help another man's son, and then it ended up saving my son's life.

Life has a funny way of bringing things back into your life. Would you believe that in 2006 one of our favorite places to sing was a Hearing Impaired Facility? It is true, and when we sign the old song "I'll Fly Away" the audience will do the sign for flying by flapping their arms like a bird's wing. I didn't learn that in school, but God knew I would need it over 20 years later.

CHAPTER SEVEN

LIFE'S UNIQUE PATHS

It is amazing how we are prepared for things that we will later use in ministry. When my wife went to college she studied Funeral Service Education, never knowing years later after she had become a cosmetologist, then becoming involved with me in Assisted Living Facilities and Nursing Homes that it would all tie together.

We met one little lady who had requested my wife to do her hair, nails, and makeup for her funeral. Well that day came. I did her funeral service and my wife did all that she had requested. As people passed by for viewing they would say, "Oh, what a beauty." Knowing that little woman as we did, those words would have made dying worth it for her. I thought now she can go on to see her beloved husband that had gone on years before, and when he saw her she would be as gorgeous as the day he left.

Speaking of beauty, there was another woman that called my wife to come to her home and do her hair. This particular woman would go for long periods of time between appointments because she never felt beautiful. Her husband would tell her how he thought she was beautiful; my wife said she had never seen anyone get literally spitting mad before, and then go into a rage because she felt so ugly. After a little time had passed she finally shared something she had never told before. As a little girl her mother would tell her how ugly and worthless she was and that she was not wanted or loved, just "in the way." At the age of 9 her mother had told her that she wanted to abort her but the doctor said that if he did that he would have to slit the throats of the other children as well since there was so little money for food and clothes. Enraged by what the doctor said, she told this innocent child that she lived only to save the others that were wanted. This woman asked, "How can I be beautiful, when I'm not wanted?" Once again this gave my wife a chance to talk to her as she held this pained woman in her arms sobbing with her as she revealed the truth of God's love for her; and that she was wanted by Him as well as thought of as a beautiful creation and that was no mistake.

I don't think they teach you that in Beauty School, but God sure loves it when we are kind to one another.

THE IMPORTANCE OF LIFE AND DEATH

I was in a place of business one day talking to the owner about the upholstery trade, when an old fella stopped in to tell his friend (the owner) of the new car he was test driving. This old guy and I had met a few times before and enjoyed talking about Notre Dame Football with each other. Well after sharing his news he went back out to the parking lot to continue his testing. I had noticed about 15-20 minutes later that the car was still there and told the owner. He said he knew and that the guy just wanted to tell him about all the bells and whistles of the car; but when the next half hour past, I noticed that the car was still there. I said, "Man that car is still out there!" The owner jumped up and said, "I sure hope that S.O.B. hasn't died on me!!" We both ran outside to see what had happened, and sure enough that old fella had died. He was sitting up in the car as if he had just fallen asleep. The owner cursed again and said, '"Now the police and EMT's are going to be here. It'll probably take hours to get this mess cleaned up!" All he could think of was, "This is going to cost me business this afternoon, because people won't come in with this going on!!" Once again someone saying ~"*What's in it for me?*"

I happened to know that the old man was a millionaire and wanted to come by later to offer the young business man financial backing on some properties around his business. Once, however, he knew the old man was gone; he had no use for him and just having his body removed from his parking lot was an aggravation.

As I look back on that afternoon, I realize that I was one of the last people on earth to speak to the old fella. I'm not like some ministers that say they hate doing funerals. I am very different from that. I am not happy that someone died and I see the tears of the family left behind. Oh, I have had some heart breaking funerals, but what I am always glad for is to know I was the last person on earth to have something to do or say about their life.

I have realized many times the sermon I preached was the last some people ever heard. When we go back to the Assisted Living Facilities and Nursing Homes where we are booked each month or so; almost always there is someone that has passed away since the last time we were there. So every time we sing, play, and share our stories of encouragement; we know by the next time there is a good chance someone will be gone. So my wife and I many times are the last ones to tell some old Mother or Father that God loves them, sing a song for them, pray for them and we are the last ones to hear them say…

"Please don't forget us…"
"Please come back…"

We have had so many tell us, "I wish they would give you two a room here, and then you could sing and play every day for us." Many times my wife and I would look at each other and say, "We would like that too!" Then we remember that there is one more place down the Highway and one more Mom, Dad, or Grandparent that will hear for the last time, "God loves you!" Oh yes, many times we are the last to hear them say how much they love their families, because after we are gone and before the family gets back to see them, they have passed away.

CHAPTER EIGHT

LOVING WHAT WE DO

We have played and sang in many parts of the country. We had a radio broadcast and a television program that aired in three states. Our program ran at different times, anywhere from 10 am to 3 am. There would be times where someone would call at the wee hours of the morning, since our phone number was displayed to do so. They would call just to say they were watching it and wanted us to know how much they loved it: after thanking them we would laugh and go back to sleep knowing that we were being used around the clock.

We have played to standing room only, and we have played for one, yes one person. It was a Sunday afternoon in Michigan when we arrived at this particular facility to be informed by the director that the dates had been turned around and that most of the people had left for another event.

Embarrassed by the mix up he apologized, gave us the donation and asked if we would come back the following month.

However, there was one woman that was sitting there ready for us to play. She had such a child like look of anticipation and enthusiasm that we knew we just couldn't take the chance of disappointing her. This was possibly our last opportunity to tell her that Jesus loves her.

So we unpacked all of our equipment, the keyboard, sound system, mic stand, music stand, CD player, everything. We then proceeded to sing and play for her and she sang with us. It was as if there were a thousand there. In all the places we have gone, that remains one of the most memorable Sunday afternoons of them all. When she sang, she sang with all her heart; and my wife put her arms around her, hugged her and told her that she was loved.

I don't believe those things just happen. So many times in the Bible we find Jesus dealt with one person at a time:

Nicodemus ~ who came to Him at night
The Rich Young Ruler
The Woman at the Well

So you see a one on one situation is something special.

MR. PARKER

I remember a man in one of the first facilities my wife and I went to. At that time we went every Monday evening. This facility had two buildings, one for more independent folks, and the other for those with Alzheimer's. We learned very quickly here that Monday was a good night, so as not to interrupt their Bingo (we have had fun with that since). Oh how we fell in love with those people.

In the second group there was a man who came and sat on the sofa just to our right. He had one hand over his face and sat there with his eyes closed, never uttering a word, never making a sound. I had wondered if he got anything out of what we were trying to do. After weeks of the same quiet, as if he were in a sleep position, one night we were singing "Amazing Grace". All of a sudden I heard a beautiful baritone voice I had never heard before there. It sounded like Jim Nabors. When I looked to my right this man was singing every word of every verse. "When we've been there ten thousand years…" My wife and I looked at each other and just smiled. We had never heard a sound from this man when we were done singing that song, he went back into position; hand over face, eyes closed, no sound, and no movement until the nurse came to take him to his room. A few weeks went by and we didn't see him anywhere. I asked the nurse where this man was. She smiled and replied, "Oh, Mr. Parker passed away a couple weeks ago. You do know he was a retired minister." I felt such emotions go through me at that time I could hardly keep from laughing out loud. "A PREACHER?!!", I said. Well that explains what happened that last night we saw him and heard him sing "Amazing Grace". I just have to believe Mr. Parker thought he was back in church again, maybe a Sunday night service like he had held over the years, getting ready to preach again like he had a thousand times before. So before he went "HOME", he wanted to sing "Amazing grace ~ how sweet the sound!", one more time. I wasn't asked to preach his funeral, but I sure would have been glad to do it!

So now when I tell this story, I always say that one of the first people I want to see when I get to heaven after Jesus will be old Reverend Parker. His eyes won't be closed or his hand covering his face, but maybe we'll be able to once again sing together as we did on that cold snowy winter night ~ "Amazing Grace". I think the three of us are going to be a heavenly trio.

Once again I am reminded that we were the last people he would hear sing, to hear pray, and to hear that "God loves you".

SPARROW

There are so many stories like Mr. Parker's. I remember one when we were in an Ohio Assisted Living Facility. That night as we began to sing I noticed a nurse had brought into the room a woman on a hospital bed: laying flat on her back the lady next to her propped her head with a pillow as we began to sing. I must admit, I wondered why they would bring someone in such a helpless condition to the music room. Then my wife began to sing that wonderful song, "His Eye Is On The Sparrow", and we went on with our program. After we had finished that night, we walked through the crowd as we always do greeting and thanking them for allowing us to sing for them: when I had gotten to the woman lying in the hospital bed she smiled really big. The lady that was sitting with her said, "When your wife sang 'His Eye Is On The Sparrow' this woman said *sparrow*. She hasn't spoken a word in years. She had a stroke. I was her neighbor and I come often to visit her."

When my wife sang, this was something that probably took her back to years ago; maybe singing it herself in church, but something happened that night and we will never forget that experience. So every time now that my wife sings that song, my mind goes back to that little lady that just said, "Sparrow".

<u>THE CALLING</u>

One afternoon just outside Chicago, we were again singing and playing as we love to do. My eyes seemed to stop on one man that was sitting to the left of where we had our equipment set up. This was a distinguished looking man, somewhere in his mid to late 50's. He seemed to be crying and wiping the tears away in a silent sort of way that would just tear your heart out. He seemed to know the words to all the songs, but I would see his lips quiver. He could only sing a few words, and then wipe his eyes much like a little boy would do. He just sat by himself, looking out the big glass windows that went around the room, and silently wiped away another tear.

After our program, as I began tearing down our equipment, I walked over to where he was sitting and shook hands with him as he was telling me his name. I told him I couldn't help but see how emotional he had been. Then with the tears flowing down his face, he began to tell me how as a young man he had been called to the ministry and how things in life seemed to take him in other directions. Yes, he knew all the songs. He also knew what it was in life he was supposed to do, but he never answered the call to the ministry. Now he was sick, unable to ever make a living and now had to live in a Nursing Home.

I wonder how many people live day after day knowing there was a call on their life and they never answered it. I come from a family of 5 boys and 1 girl. I am the oldest boy and my mother use to say, "Son, don't lower yourself to become President of the United States when you have been called to be a minister for God."

CHAPTER NINE

HOMELESS:
MORE THAN STREET PEOPLE

We were asked about two years ago if we would come to Key West Florida at Thanksgiving. Key West at Thanksgiving?!!! I guess so!!!! Our guests not only invited us to dinner, but to help feed the homeless. Homeless in Key West Florida? Yes, homeless in Key West.

Many times I have driven through the Upper Keys and over the 7 mile Bridge gazing at the green/blue water on both sides of the road as it narrows toward Key West. Sports cars, boats, we've seen it all; but homeless? We met with the people that had called for us to come and they tried to tell us what to expect that next day. I never would have believed it; homeless, helpless, such sad faces, story after story. We met one man that was one of the top executives of a Fortune 500 Company. Things in life had gotten so bad because of bad choices, that his wife had committed suicide. He lost everything. This is when we realized and learned a new term "White Collar Homeless".

I don't know exactly what the National Average is today, but I have heard that most people are only 2 paychecks away from being in the streets. In fact, many of the people we meet and talk to in the Assisted Living Facilities and Nursing Homes tell us they have lost their homes. No matter how beautiful the surroundings are (and there are some so beautiful that we feel as if we are in the Opryland Hotel or some kind of beautiful resort) to them they had to leave their home. It's not just brick and mortar, but the memories of their life. I mentioned earlier in the book;

mine is the Old Coolspring Place; for my wife it's her home on 20 acres of woods and gardens. I believe everyone has their own memory and I know these people sure do.

This is why we do what we do, because for an hour or so each afternoon or evening these people forget about their disappointments. My wife always asks, "How many remember 'Sing Along with Mitch Miller?' Well we are the gospel version, except we don't have the red bouncing ball! So come on and sing along with us!" They smile and laugh and we all take that little trip down memory lane to a day before walkers, wheelchairs, and canes. We see their faces light up when we sing "Yes, Jesus Loves Me...", "The B.I.B.L.E...", or "Onward Christian Solider". There is something about music, especially gospel music.

While we were rolling in our equipment at one facility; we passed a little lady walking down the hall. I noticed that she wasn't just walking, but she was pacing, up and back and up and back as if she couldn't be still. When we began to sing, she came in and sat by the back door without a movement, with her eyes fixed on us the whole time until the program was over. Then she stood up and began to pace once again. As I passed her taking the equipment out to the car (and made quite a few trips at that) she would say to me each time, "Wonderful. That was wonderful.", and kept on pacing never to miss a beat. It is amazing what might seem small to us, turns on a light for them. One church gave me some of their old song books (you know the one with the Hymns) they were not using, so we could pass them out so that it might be easier for them to sing along. Well I guess I don't have to tell you that each person wanted one for them-selves. Sometimes there were so many people; we had to ask them if they wouldn't mind sharing. As they received their book, they held it, looked through it and just smiled as to have found a long lost friend.

When we asked them, as they would leaf through the hymns, if anyone has a favorite they would like to sing. They all have their favorites. I believe in their minds they, like Rev. Parker, are back in a wonderful church service again.

One old fellow asked me, "Do you ever do the 'Our Father?'" I answered yes. He smiled and told me that when we do that it reminded him of going to church with his mother when he was just a boy. One of the highlights of our program is when we sing the "Lord's Prayer". I guess I think of those years and miles ago when Mr. Mac said, "Just play and sing for them son. They will love it."

I read somewhere that there are three things that will take our minds back to years ago ~ music, smell, and taste.

THERE IS JUST SOMETHING ABOUT MUSIC

I heard the story about the great baseball player Ted Williams. One of his closest friends was Dominic DiMaggio (the brother of Joe DiMaggio). Ted and Dom (as Ted called him) went to Florida to see his old friend for what turned out to be the last time. Dominic had a beautiful baritone voice. He told Ted that he wanted to sing him a song. It is about two guys that were very close friends. Dom sang the song. As weak as Ted was, he clapped his hands and smiled. So Dom sang it again. He promised Ted he would call each day to tell him the scores of the Red Socks games. He did call a few times giving the scores to the nurse to pass on to Ted. One day Ted answered the phone and said, "Hi Dom!" Those were the last words he ever heard from his old friend.

The beautiful part of this story for me is that Dom sang a song for his friend. Again this was the last song he ever heard, but it brought a smile. As sick as Ted was, he clapped his hand as if to say, "Thanks ole buddy." Yes there is just something about music.

What makes this story so special to me is remembering the first television game I ever saw as a young boy. Dominic DiMaggio was playing that day.

YOUTHFUL INNOCENTS

I have noticed at some of the places we go; the people are allowed pets. Those that have dogs love to pet them as they "stroll around the block". You can tell the dogs love it too as they stride with pride such as a King or Queen would during an important state of pomp and circumstance.

I love to tell the story of a Christmas when my brother (18 months younger) and I were given a beautiful little black Cocker Spaniel with long floppy ears. I was about 9 years old and little brother about 7 ½. All we knew was that we had a Cocker Spaniel Dog, and we were so proud. Any dog we ever had before was just a dog, but now we had a Cocker Spaniel! So after Christmas dinner, we thought it would be a good idea to take our dog for a walk. Coats, hats, and out the door we went with a little rope around his neck. Man, we were so proud. As we walked the little guy down the street two teenage boys saw us. As they approached us they said, "Boys ~ that's a fine looking dog you have there." We replied, "Yea! We got him this morning for Christmas!" One of them asked us, "What is it, a male or a female?" I looked at my brother and he looked at me. At the same time we said, "Man ~ it's neither one. Can't you see it's a Cocker Spaniel?!!" They said, "Oh yea, we can see that."

I don't know if kids are that innocent today with T.V., etc...; but when I tell that story it always gets a laugh. They also have wonderful stories in which they love to share with us. I believe their animals help them remember a time many, many years ago. There is no pet that can ever take the place of a person that will go visit these people; just let them talk of all the things of years ago.

LOVE AND COMPANIONSHIP ~ WE ALL NEED IT

I heard of a woman that would call Time & Temperature just to hear someone's voice. What no one could tell her, was that the voice was electronic, not a real person at all.

I have also heard of experiments with animals where they have held and loved them, rubbed and talked to them gently and lovingly; then to another group they did just the opposite, totally ignoring them except for food. The results: the first group grew and did well; the second didn't grow much and had many problems. I believe there are people who need to have someone put their arm around them so they know that they are loved.

I saw a sign in front of a church which read, "If you're looking for a sign from God ~ this is it! Come to church." I would say if you are listening for God to tell you what to do; go help the people in the Nursing Homes and Assisted Living Facilities. I believe God has lead you to read this book so He can speak to you ~ **GO!!** Hear the words we hear from these people, "Please don't forget us. Why don't you come more often?"

Often I have said we wouldn't let people talk about us the way we talk about ourselves:

I have no talent~
I can't sing~
I can't help anyone~

the list goes on with I can't, I can't, I can't..., but if someone else was telling all what we <u>could not</u> do I believe most people would stop them and say, "Wait a minute!! I can do things to help someone!"

This reminds me of the movie "Schindler's List". During W.W. II, Oskar Shchindler tried to help the Jews by saving them from the Nazi's. At the end of the movie he is crying because he couldn't save anymore. He felt that if he had only sold his ring, he could have saved more Jew's. If only he could have sold_____, he could have saved <u>one more</u> Jew. That is why we have booked and book places to go play and sing, because maybe <u>one more</u> person will turn to Jesus Christ.

CHAPTER TEN

BUILDING ALTARS

My hope is to challenge everyone who reads this book to do something to make someone's life better. At times we become involved in things and we wonder are we doing any good, or is this really what I am supposed to do? Someone said if you want to see God smile, tell Him your plans. We must sound like our children when they say that when they grow up they'll be an astronaut, a great doctor, or a famous musician, and we just smiled.

One of my brothers was pastoring a wonderful church in Florida. They were building a new addition, and I first got involved by reupholstering the platform pews and the new building was a multipurpose facility. I had to set up chairs then take them down for every service, because it was also the basketball court, the dining hall, and the concert auditorium. I had worked out a system for setting up the chairs for each activity.

One day I was wheeling load after load of chairs into and around the massive floor putting them in place. All of a sudden I found myself asking the Lord, "Is this what you really want me to be doing? I can preach, play all different musical instruments. Why, a lot of people have told me I was their favorite singer." In fact I was telling the Lord just what a bargain He had in me. Then I heard Him speak to my heart in that gentle, soft way. I felt Him say, "You're not setting up chairs; you're building altars. People are going to come in here and hear the gospel preached. They are going to hear beautiful music. There are going to be husbands and wives that are going to dedicate their lives to living right.

Their marriages will be reconciled. There will be children getting involved and growing up in the way they should. There are people going to be healed of their sicknesses. So you see you really are building altars."

After that, each time I put the chairs in place, I prayed that, "...whoever sits here today, God You will meet whatever need they have and their family also." On my last Sunday before leaving the church, I told this story. Person after person came to me and said, "I want to take over that job. I want to build altars."

So the job you are doing today may not seem important. You may be feeling as I was that day, but if you will be faithful over a few things, the Bible says, He will make you ruler over many. (Matthew 25:21) By the way, my wife and I continued the practice of praying for those who would come to church. We would walk and pray around the pews, and even pick a different seat each week.

I like to think of it as giving a cup of cold water. Matthew 10:42 tell us that if we do what might seem small compared to other ministries; we will not lose our reward. One of my favorite songs says, "...If just a cup of water I place within your hand, then just a cup of water is all that I demand." Don't you think it's time to give back that cup of water?

OUT OF AFRICA

A woman in one of my churches said to me, "Pastor, I could never tell God that I'd go where He wanted me to go, because I am sure He would send me to Africa." Looking at me with tremendous fear in her eyes she said, "I don't want to go to Africa." I patted her on her shoulder and replied, "My dear sister, of all the people in the world for God to send; I can't think of anyone less qualified to go. You don't know anything about Africa, and all God wants you to give is that cup of water He placed in your hand." She looked as if a ton had been lifted off her shoulders as she smiled and sighed with relief.

This story reminds me of a song I wrote years ago:

Lord help me today, you know what I need,
Only You be the judge of that.
For You know where I'm going,
You know where I've been,
You alone know where I'm at.

Some things I have asked for,
some things I have got,
Now I'd like to give some of them back.

So help me today, You know what I need,
Only You be the judge of that.

God has something in mind for all of us. We just have to let Him be the judge of what is best for us, and then allow Him to be our mentor.

THE MENTOR

Two sportscasters were talking about many of the interviews they had with the different football players. One mentioned a young man who had come from an extremely hard background. Crime all around, drugs everywhere he turned, many of his friends in prison; but they said his coach in

High School had helped him stay focused and he went to college.

His college coach continued the hard work with him. He had helped the player three different times. Picking him up, dusting him off, and each time the sportscasters said, "What a wonderful thing that the coach didn't give up on him, but he mentored him through his four years of college." One interviewer laughed and said, "It is so amazing now. When you interview this young football star; it is like talking to his coach, because he has followed the things he is supposed to do."

I thought as I heard that program, that is what it is like when we follow Christ. When people talk to us they begin to see Jesus. It sounds like Jesus is speaking, because he is our mentor. So when we go to the Nursing Homes and Assisted Living Facilities, it is an extension of God's hands and arms. When we pat or hug one of his people and tell them "God loves you"; He is our mentor, so therefore we sound like Him.

Most of these people can't go out to a church service anymore, so we never hear anyone say, "I didn't feel like coming tonight." In my years of pastoring churches, I have heard over, and over, "Oh I just didn't feel like coming today (tonight)." In fact there was a wonderful lady in one of our churches that hadn't been in service for quite a few weeks. When the day came that she did make it, I went straight to her and said, "I am so glad you're here this morning!", and proceeded to let her know how much she was missed. She looked me square in the eye and replied, "Oh Pastor! I couldn't be here because I was so sick. Why I barely made it three or four times this week to Walmart." There are not a lot of times I don't have something to say in response, but this was one of those rare moments in life when I just shook my head and walked away toward the platform.

My brother (next to me in age) on the left, and myself with our rifles ready to help in war effort.

This is a V-mail from one of my Uncles overseas during the war.

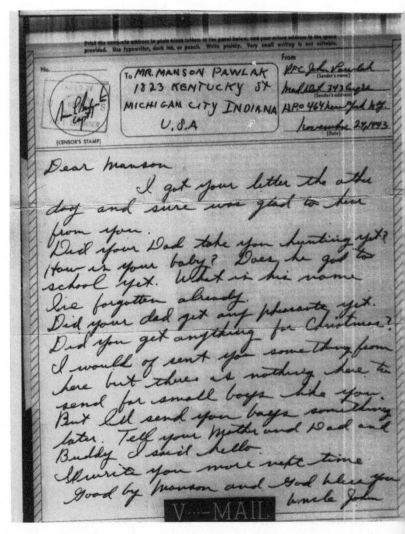

Mr. Mac is on the left with some
friends after a meeting.

Lake Michigan ~ one of my favorite places &
"My Old Friend".

Some family photos, The Rice's ~ Uncle Fred (the fabulous musician), Grandma (famous waffle iron), Grandpa (the pastor & church builder).

Grandpa & Grandma Pawlak's Wedding Picture.
Taken some time shortly after the
turn of the century.

Great Grandma and Great Grandpa Pawlak.
Grandpa Casimir middle, Aunt Hattie left,
Uncle Steve on lap.

Last picture of us all at the Old Coolspring Place,
I'm wearing the black shirt with white jacket.
(Oldest of six)

Some of our friends from around the country,
one is warming by the fireside.

The Hearing Impaired is singing (signing)
along with us in the "Buckeye" State.

From chapter twelve ~ "Booked and Broke"
Leigh Ann is getting things ready just before
getting dressed for an Assisted Living Facility.

Our car became a mirage of a house;
much too small, but it kept us from saying,
"My God I am homeless!"

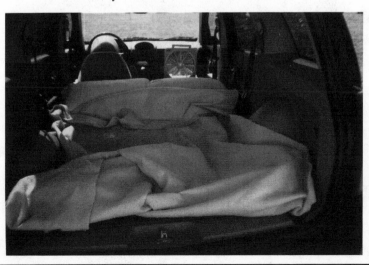

CHAPTER ELEVEN

NO ROOM FOR EGOS

I have found that <u>the ministry will keep you humble.</u> Quite often when I have delivered my sermon, I felt confident that I really "rang the bell" this time. I no more get to the back of the church to shake hands with the people as they were leaving, when someone will say, "Pastor, it seemed like you were struggling this morning, like you were having a hard time." When I felt as if I just preached the poorest sermon in my life the response has been, "Pastor I believe that was the best sermon you've ever preached!"

I recall a Sunday morning service years ago, my wife and I had sung, others had special music, it seemed so good. As I was preaching I noticed a young man sitting to my right. He was sitting on the edge of the pew as if he were clinging onto every word I had spoken. Well, I don't have to tell you that inspired me to tell some of my greatest stories to a point I didn't really want to stop preaching; but for time sake I had to bring the service to a close. While the final prayer was being prayed by one of the Deacons, I moved very quietly down the aisle to the back door, once again to shake hands, and to speak to each person. When the boy's grandmother came along in line I said, "Well, it sure looked like your grandson enjoyed the sermon today." I had mentioned to her about him sitting on the edge of the pew the whole time. Then the grandmother replied, "Oh no, it wasn't your sermon. My grandson has back trouble and he can't sit all the way back in the seat, because it would cause him too much pain." So as I related this story to my wife at lunch that day; we both smiled at each other and agreed that the ministry will certainly keep you humble.

"THE MISSION FIELD"
AT HOME OR ABROAD

When I was a young man I dreamed of going all over the world to preach, play, and sing. Sometimes our dreams come true, but in a way we don't expect. I wasn't able to travel the world over, so God brought the people from other countries to me. Through the Nursing Homes and Assisted Living Facilities right here in this country, we have been able to minister to many who have moved from their home country to the U.S.A. Now here they sit right in front of us so that we may play and sing telling them of the love that Christ has for them, even when some of their religions don't believe in Christ.

I had an idea for a Christian cartoon with a mountain and two men, one on each side. Each man was praying for God to send him over that mountain to tell those people on the other side about Him. The moral of the story: if each man would stay where he was, God could use him on his own side of the mountain.

I loved when missionaries came to our church when I was a boy. They brought big round rolls of film of their adventures as a missionary. Each one that came told their story and I would think maybe that is where I will go someday. They showed pictures of elephants, tigers, lions, and thousands of people with black shiny skin, no shoes, and limited clothing. At the end of the film, as you could hear the projector run a little louder as the reel was spinning, the missionary would so often say in a loud booming voice, "So we leave as the sun sets on the Serengeti…" That beautiful golden sunset and again an elephant in the background with towering African palm trees that looked like they went all the way to Heaven, I would say someday I am going to see that sunset over the Serengeti. Well that hasn't happened yet, I keep thinking someday.

CHAPTER TWELEVE

BOOKED AND BROKE

The dictionary defines *bookings* as a scheduled performance, but *broke* just three words ~ **OUT OF MONEY**.

I mentioned in an earlier chapter that we had booked ourselves into about 50 Assisted Living Facilities. We had been working for a man that had heart problems, and was not able to do the work himself. We found ourselves in a unique situation. If we worked hard and got the furniture out as fast as we could, we ran ourselves out of things to do, but we were now running out of money. We had already sold all of our furniture, and anything else we had to stay afloat. We were on the road, living in Motel rooms trying to do our Assisted Living work, as well as whatever work we could do.

The way it is set up with these facilities is that after you sing and play for them, then you turn in a receipt for their donations from their corporate office, but it could take 6-8 weeks before we received a check. There were some that never sent a thing. Our hearts would break for those places that had nothing to help us with, but we never turned one place down because they couldn't support us.

Now things were becoming desperate. We rented a small storage unit so we could change our clothes and unload our mats and covers that we used for a bed at night in the back of our SUV. By this time we had no money for Motel rooms anymore, so we had to begin to live out of our car; plus the air conditioner went out, of course it's JULY!

I had heard of people living out of their cars, but never could I have imagined this would happen to us. We went to a store and found a fan used for camping that ran off of batteries. We would prop it up in the front of the car and try to get just a little air. Boy, those eight batteries ran down so fast. Often we couldn't afford to replace them. So in those hot July and August nights we would walk around a Rest Area, or back lot of a big Truck Plaza until we could try to get a few hours of sleep. A couple of these Plazas had showers that we could use for $5. One of them was kind enough to let us both shower for the price of one since we were married. Another one had a young lady; about due any minute it seemed to have her baby, who would always hand us our $5 back when we turned our towels in. The blessing in this is that we could then go to McDonald's and split a breakfast. This is when I began to appreciate "Senior Coffee".

Sometimes we weren't able to get into a shower so we either used the Rest Area restrooms to clean up and get dressed, or the storage unit to change our clothes. Then we hoped and prayed that we had enough gas to get to the next Assisted Living Facility or Nursing Home one more day.

There were things that happened in those Rest Areas that made us wonder if our ministry would end that night. One night a group of people drunk out of their minds, pulled up next to our SUV; cursing and swearing with their bottles in their hands, we waited for them to start fighting or shooting each other. We laid there to scared to move. Our eyes opening and shutting was the only way anyone would have known we were even alive.

I thought if I tried to jump to the front seat to drive out of there, they might grab our keys, or I'd even get over-powered by those drunken crazed young guys, and they could grab my beautiful wife. That was more than I could bear. So we laid there praying for God to please get us out of there alive. I was not called up to go to war, but I thought this must have been something like others felt in a fox hole, or pinned down in a building during the war with people running all over, voices you've never heard before in your life. I thought, "Where are the police now? I know they come through these places every hour, but where are they now?" In their drunken state they finally got into their car, doors slamming against ours. We laid there still trying not to breath too deep, not to cough, not to make a sound, spinning tires finally drove off to enter the Highway. We prayed that they didn't crash into some poor innocent family out on the Interstate.

Relieved that we were safe, we moved a few places down to try to finish some kind of rest, not believing we would have anymore problems, because we were being extra cautious. A few nights later; however, we had another visitor around 3 am pounding on our windows. This time it's a drug addict, asking for money to fix his car that he said was broke down on the Interstate. We knew he just needed another fix, or drink, or both. This time I did jump into the front seat and drove down the Highway to who knows where. Then we saw a gas station that was open all night. We pulled in and stopped, put our heads into our hands saying, "How in the world did this happen?" We decided that we'd better stay where it would be safer, such as a Truck Plaza or 24 hour Walmart, some place that had better lighting, security, and an all night restroom.

After giving all we had to give for this ministry, the day came that we could no longer go on any further. We now had less than $5 on us, and our hearts were broken. We didn't even have the gas to take a ride down by the lake, where we had always gone to try and figure out what we could possibly do. We were now four car payments behind and there was nowhere left for us, but the streets.

So I called our Son in the Washington D.C. area. There was a contact person for us to see. They had promised my wife a job with FEMA. I said I would get work with an upholstery shop somewhere, but we were broke. I knew nothing else to do except to take all of our musical equipment to a Pawn Shop, and try to get enough money to go out East.

When I started as a young boy with Mr. Mac, I just played the guitar. Now we had a keyboard with all the background instruments and rhythms, etc... My wife sometimes used background CD's and Cassettes to sing with. We tried to take the best sound possible to these precious people, we had our own CD's also; but that day we pulled up to the Pawn Shop and unloaded <u>everything</u> (keyboard, mic stand, music stand, p.a. system), every piece of equipment we had; just to see if we could get enough money to make that trip East and get some work. My poor wife didn't know how the pawn shop system worked. She thought we were losing everything that day. So while she was crying, I hugged her and said, "OH NO HONEY! We will come back and get it when we have made some money out East."

So we got the money and signed the pawn ticket, then they took our finger prints and all the legal things that go with it. As we pulled away and drove back to our 10x10 storage unit to pick up our few clothes; I felt my heart was going to explode out of my body. My wife began to call and cancel our bookings, she dialed and cried trying to explain to the directors that we had to go out East, and wouldn't be able to come to their facility. Sometimes she would say to me, "Honey, will you talk to this one?", and with tears streaming down her face she would smile and hand me the phone and always say, "Thank you."

In three days we were out East, looking forward to making some money, but by the time we got there FEMA put a freeze on hiring. There we were again, no job and our pawn money nearly gone. I did, however, find an upholstery shop that a man had opened in what had been an 1850's Black Church. He put us to work the next day. We worked together on furniture. My wife sews very well also, and we did what we call "tag team'n" the jobs. The man was great to work for, but he didn't know how fast we would catch him up, and out of work we would be again. So I called the man back North that had the heart problems and by this time he needed help again, as the song says, "On the road again."

Once again, within a few weeks we were out of work. I had a friend in Florida that I hadn't talked to in a long time. I called him, and he put me in contact with a man that invited us to come there and go to work for him. Within two weeks I realized I couldn't do the things that his 20 & 30 years old workers were doing. He was a great guy, but he felt the same as I did. My wife and I were offered a job we could do together, and came North once again. It turned out to be the best job we could have gotten at the time. It was very low pay, but like everything else when we put our pay together things began to happen within a very short time. We completely paid our car to date, as well as everything else.

I knew these were some of the darkest days of our lives. I know our families talked amongst themselves and thought we had lost our minds. They must have thought we were crazy. However, God called us to do a work. Now when I see our mic stand and other pieces of equipment that still has the bright yellow pawn sticker on them, I smile. I thought at first of taking them off, but I left them there as a reminder, a sign; that if we put God first He will never fail us.

I do believe that God put a protection around our minds during those days and nights. We have talked many times of the miracles, that we never got sick, the few things we did have never wore out. We felt like the children of Israel going through the wilderness. Some years ago I felt

God speak to me in that soft gentle way that He uses. The question was could I put Him first in my life. As I examined that idea I had to be truthful. I knew that I had not always put Him first, but I said, "Lord I will do my best to make You #1 from now on." Looking back, I believe I can say my wife and I have put God #1 in our lives. If it took all we went through, and if telling our story helps one person, then it's worth it. If it challenges someone while reading this book to say, "I want to work in an Assisted Living Facility/Nursing Home." <u>It is really worth it!!</u>

CHAPTER THIRTEEN

BRINGING OUT THE LIGHT

We had just pulled into Baltimore, Maryland. It was late afternoon, and we were looking forward to the next day to see if there was any record that would tell us of the day my Grandfather, along with his Mother, had reached the shores of this wonderful country. As I mentioned in an earlier chapter this is where my family came to the U.S., not as so many others that came through Ellis Island in New York's Harbor.

We checked into a nice hotel on the edge of town thinking about the Crab Cakes we would feast on the next day; but as we settled into our room, after showers, etc…; I believe God brought something to my attention. There on the dresser was everything we would need (so it was stated) to make our stay with them enjoyable, menus listing Pizza to Prime Rib, a list of all the attractions we wouldn't want to miss during our stay, the channel changer, beautiful towels, extra pillows, and all the toiletries one could imagine. All of a sudden like a bomb went off, I thought where is the Bible?! Yes the Bible, the one that the Gideons place in all of the Hotel/Motel rooms! I jumped up from the bed, pulled open the drawer of the nightstand, and there it was hidden away in the dark. I thought this isn't right! This is the Light and we must bring it out! A lamp unto my feet and a light unto my pathway the writer called it. Before we left our room the next morning, we called the Manager and asked him if he would please leave the Bible out from now on. When we asked one Manager of a Motel to leave the Bible out; he replied that he didn't want to offend anyone that might not be a Christian. We mentioned to him that we also had paid to stay there, and that we were offended that the Bible wasn't visible as every-thing else was, and that it helps so many, but if someone didn't want to look at it they didn't have to any more than a person would have to look at anything else in the room. He did say he would consider our rebuttal, and think about it. When we go to places that do have the Bible out in plain view, we thank them for doing so, and encourage those in the Assisted Living Facilities and Nursing Homes to read their Bibles or play the Bible tapes.

I met a woman one day that told me how proud she was of the condition of her Bible. She said, "I have had it about 20-25 years and it looks brand new!" I replied, "Shame on you. By this time it should be tattered and worn from being used." This reminds me of an old song we used to sing years ago called "Dust on the Bible", it goes a little like this:

Dust on the Bible, dust on God's Holy Word,
The word's of all the Prophets and the
sayings of our Lord
Of all the other books you'll find there's
none salvation holds
Get the dust off the Bible and redeem your poor soul.

There is something so powerful about the Bible that goes beyond words. I remember a time years ago in my life that I was going through something that often I felt I couldn't always sit down and read. At night many times trying to sleep I would reach to the nightstand and get my Bible just to hold it to my chest. I would perspire so hard that by holding my Bible to me that the beautiful green cover faded until it has brown spots and streaks on it; all the different colors from becoming so wet. I couldn't pray some eloquent prayer during the night, just held tight that old Bible to my chest until I fell asleep. Then once again the sun would bring its light into my room and awaken me to another day. Then the whole process would begin again; but holding that Bible to my chest was God's way of bringing out the Light to me.

So you see that is why the first thing we do when we are on the road and walk into a Motel room is to look for those beautiful Gideon Bibles and set them out where they belong, in plain view. This allows it to bring out the Light to the next traveler that will enter the room. If you would like to hear more stories of what has happened because of the Gideons placing these Bibles in these rooms, contact your local Gideon and they will send a wonderful speaker to your church. WOW!! What stories! When I was pastoring one of the top Sundays on our church calendar was when a Gideon was coning to speak. He would tell over and over how the Bible brought out the Light. So we sing and play because the music is always calling us back to another Facility, but my wife and I live our lives and ministry by the words from Psalm 127:1

Except the Lord built the house
They labor in vain that built it...

A woman heard me use that scripture so often that she made me a plaque for my desk. This will be the first thing you see if you were to walk into our small home office today.

So the next Motel, Hotel, Hospital Room, or Doctor's Office you're in, find these beautiful Bibles and put them where they belong because to a dark room and a dark world they are the brightest Lights of all.

CHAPTER FOURTEEN

FIRST IMPRESSIONS

I believe one of the greatest things we can inherit from our family is the stories they tell us. In the Assisted Living and Nursing Homes there is always someone that tugs on our sleeve to say, "Let me tell you a story." They tell us something their parents told them; for me I loved to hear the stories my Dad told of his days on the railroad, or the night shifts he worked as a baker. I loved to hear of his days as a young man in the Mountains of California clearing fire trails. He was in what was called the C.C.C. (Civilian Conservation

Corps), and how he and our Uncle built their great <u>Box Kites</u>. He described how they took long pieces of very thin wood, tied and glued them together, and then took <u>News Papers</u> to form the perfect box shape for their kite. Often from a hilltop they launched their own "Hindenburg" for what would be the 1st transatlantic flight of a Box Kite. If the string were to break, Dad would tell how they would bring the string of their kite through their bedroom window, tie it to a chair, or dresser drawer handle so they could fly it all night long. If they got up during the night or the first thing in the morning, they would pull on the string. How he would smile as he told us, "It was still there." So making us boys a kite was something he loved second only to his fishing. I have thought of the things we as Christians need during the night. When we need a string to pull on to feel God is still there, and how happy we are when we feel that small tug on the other end of our Spiritual Kite.

That brings me to a memory all the way back to the Old Coolspring Place now more than fifty years ago. It was a day made for flying, so Dad saw an opportunity to make his favorite kite ~ A

BOX KITE. Taking all the pains and patience of a surgeon, he cut, glued, and put together a kite that might have been his best effort since he and our Uncle had built one so many years ago. He smiled and said, "Let's go try it boys!" So down the long stairway we went gliding over all twenty seven steps. My brother and I carried it around the house and out in the field (that has long been filled with houses and their basket ball rimmed garages), but that day was a day that the Wright Brothers would have envied for flight. The lift off was set. Dad showed us how to let out just enough string to start running with the kite over ones head, while the other hand held the string, then with one mighty heave threw that big box skyward and let the wind carry it up and out. **Boy** what a sight!! When it got down range (as they say at NASA), we began laughing with the thoughts of how we could pull the string in our bedroom window that night.

Then somewhere beyond the knee high field grass, which was now golden and shiny, we heard a shot gun blast, then another, and with the last echo of a 12 gage down came our beautiful Box Kite, covered with papers of yesterday's news

from births to obituaries. I can still hear my Dad yell out, "Well I'll be shot!!!!!!" This time though it was our kite that had been shot right out of the sky on its maiden flight, and that was our introduction to Lou. There are so many stories I could write from those days, but I will say this, we became very close friends over the years. I learned a great lesson that we still use today:
<u>You can't go by your first impressions!!</u>

Our oldest son got a guitar for Christmas when he was about 9 years old (about the same age I was when I first started to play). However, in just a few weeks I knew he would become a much better musician than I could ever be. As he was growing up he would bring home some of the young people he was playing with, and you talk about first impressions!!

Some of these long haired kids looked like they wouldn't be able to find their way home, but when you give them a guitar and let them begin to play; I heard some of the best music I have ever heard in my life. Our first idea about someone can be so wrong. Many times my wife and I see people in our services that look like they don't care for us at all, but as we get a chance to talk to them and get to know them, they turn out to be some of our closest friends. So if you have had your kite shot out of the sky by someone, don't give up they just might turn out to be one of your closest friends.

Oh by the way, a few years ago when Lou died, I was called to do his funeral; but was in another part of the country and couldn't make it home. It still hurts today.

CHAPTER FIFTEEN

STORY SEEDS

Story seeds are not a phrase you can look up in the dictionary. Years ago a woman told me a story, and I had no idea what it would mean until disaster flooded in on us and I mean flooded. She told me of the day her little girl (less than 5 years old) was playing in the back yard of their old farm house. This child had beautiful blonde hair with long curls (some-thing like Shirley Temple in her childhood movies); her mother was working in the yard trying to make everything beautiful. All of a sudden there was a scream, that beautiful child was yelling for help. This lovely little girl had fallen head and face first into the old cesspool (this is what was used before the wonderful days of plumbing). The mother ran to pull her small daughter from that awful pit. The child now had all the dirt and waste of that cesspool covering her long blonde locks, and the smell was so bad that only a mother could throw her arms around her to brush away the falling tears. Then the mother said to the little girl, "Oh honey! I could easier make another one than to clean you up." Immediately the mother said she felt God speak to her and say, "That's how I felt about you before you came to me."

Well that story came running back into my mind like the waters that had flooded our sound equipment. I don't believe I was ever so low in all of our ups and downs, in our ministry, as I was that day. We had stored our equipment in a basement between engagements. We placed it all with such care and covered everything to keep it safe. What we didn't know was that it was right next to the water shut-off; we thought it was a gas pipe. Yes, you guessed it, somehow it began to leak and the water had come up so high that it filled our sound system speakers full of water, and our mics were filled and musty smelling. They smelled much like that first Nursing Home I mentioned in the front of the book. I thought, "Well maybe the Home Owner's Insurance will cover this mess because getting a new one would be so much easier than trying to clean all the dirt, slime and that awful smell". Then it happened, that <u>story seed</u> that was planted in my mind over forty years ago came to full bloom. It was like that little girl in the cesspool. Then I looked up toward heaven and told God, "I still want to sing for you." Then the song I sang years ago, "Tho' He Slay Me, Yet Will I Trust Him", came to me, those words Job said in the Bible. I said to my wife, "Honey, the story's not been told yet."

Well, the Insurance Company didn't replace it. So, we took that sound system, the mics and the dirty grimy electrical cords and washed, cleaned and shined everything until it sparkled. Then we took all our equipment and set it up in the living room with our keyboard, guitar stand, etc… and we said, "Now every time we walk through the living room, we will see another miracle." I am happy to say that the sound is just like brand new.

So off we go to bring out the music of hope and tell many, many more of God's great love.

So when the music begins to play, the violins blend in with the back ground voices, as well as all the other wonderful musical options we have, the listeners will never know how something that once looked so bad, dirty and horribly smelly could bring such beauty and sound; not just for the sound system, but for us because God had to clean us up as well. We were just as dirty as that little girl in the cesspool (or our sound system).

I am thankful for *Story Seeds*.

CHAPTER SIXTEEN

SMALL THINGS BRING BIG BLESSINGS

The widow's might, the five loafs and two fish, the woman's crudes of oil, and my Grandmother's waffle iron. They all have one thing in common; they were small things that brought big blessings. I only know what I read about in the Bible stories, but Grandma's waffle iron; I was there and saw it firsthand. Such pride she had when she told the stories of Tommy Zimmerman, a close preacher friend to her and my Grandpa and how proud she was every time she saw an article in a magazine or paper that Tommy had written. She would begin to tell the story as she pointed to that old waffle iron and told of how he loved those waffles that she had made on what by now looked worthless to anyone else. She wouldn't have taken any amount of money for that old memory maker. She would smile about the countless other guests that had set their feet under that table, which was always set with the dishes and cups, etc... placed upside down. This was something she had done as a girl in Kentucky. A small thing? No, not to Grandma, just big blessings.

There was a lady in another Assisted Living Facility that reminded me so much of Grandma. She told us she invented the Hair Dryer and had all the pictures and articles to prove it. She would tell us over and over the same story, until we started to sing and play those old Gospel songs. She would sit down right in front and begin to sing along with us every word. I believe she understood these old songs told a story much older than hers; but as soon as we finished with the presentation, she would start all over again by saying, "I invented the Hair Dryer." Maybe hat's why I love to sing for every group my favorite story when I sing "I Would Love to Tell You What I Think of Jesus".

Some of my greatest memories are of these people that lived such long and useful lives. Such as the night years ago I was pastoring an Indiana Country Church. It looked like something from a calendar, but this January night was cold and snowy. I was just a young kid, in my 20's, and I <u>knew</u> no matter how high the snow was, or how low the temperature got I had better be at church and have that ole potbelly stove going just in case someone tried to come to service that night. Sure enough, two people showed up and no it wasn't young people. It was a woman and her 92 year old father. So yes, I did my best to have service. I guess the old fellow knew there was just something special about braving the cold as he had for all those winters. Oh, and I think something that makes that memory special is because the old man had a son that was a preacher, as well he and his wife were great friends of my Grandparents. I just knew they had spent wonderful times together and had been guests in my Grandparent's home many times over the years and were just two more who enjoyed Grandma's waffle iron.

Some of my fondest memories are of a cold winter night with just the strong at heart that dared to come to service. In fact the very first duet with my wife was before we were even courting. It was one of those blistering cold snowy January Wednesday night services when you're not sure if anyone will show or not. Once again there were those diehards that came through practically impossible weather. There were four of us that night. We met in the small library to save on heat. I had my guitar to start the service with some hymns. We were singing "In the Garden". The next thing I knew it was just our two voices. My wife says she knew that sound that night was special. In fact it is one of our most cherished memories.

Over the years I have seen many T-shirts that read, "I Survived the Winter of 19__", or "I Survived the Snow of (year and place)". I have yet to see any T-shirts that read, "I Survived the Sunshine of Miami Beach" (or West Palm Beach). There is just something special about a cold snowy winter night. So now when we drive up to another Assisted Living Facility, and see the fire place going in side; we stomp the snow off our shoes and get ready to sing again, and hear more wonderful stories.

SOME DAY A SENIOR

We have met so many people over 100 years old in Nursing Homes and Assisted Living Facilities. There was one woman that was 103 years old. She could hear every word that was spoken, sang along with all the songs, and when she got ready to go back to her room; she stood straight up and walked away better than I could. I asked the director if she had any friends, or family that came to visit her. To my surprise I was told her daughter, who was in her 80's, came by weekly to check in on her.

"Senior's" are the fastest growing group in our country. This is something we all need to look at a bit closer than ever.

You may never be a Mother
You may never be a Father
You may never be Rich

You may never be a Home Owner, etc...etc...etc...

But if you live long enough ~ <u>You will become a</u> ~ **Senior Citizen**

If ever there was a time in our history now is the time to reach out to all the Seniors everywhere. There are too many of our churches overlooking our Seniors. They need to become more involved. Things happen to these people because they are living in a facility that they would have never experienced. They have friends they would have many times not have socialized with; most of these facilities are made up a bit like neighborhoods. So they now have neighbors they would have never lived next door to before. I see such love and caring for each other's family; and of course from time to time griping and complaining of what the other did or did not do.

One evening a while back, I was watching T.V. and there was a terrible plane crash, about 200 or so people lost their lives. They were people from all over the world, all faiths, colors, back grounds, etc... The thought came to me as I watched this report here were people that for many reasons would have never lived together, worshiped together, or even in some cases eaten together, but that day they all "died" together. We see this in facilities as well; people that would have never thought to even socialize together are now neighbors. For the most part, every week or so often in the middle of the night someone dies and goes on to stand before God. I think had they not experienced the facilities with the little new neighborhoods, and all their new friends and neighbors, those last days would have not been as complete.

CHAPTER SEVENTEEN

MORE STORIES IN OHIO

There have been so many states and places we have played and sang, and so many beautiful facilities and wonderful people we have met. There are some I have already shared with you; however, here are some more special stories that can't be forgotten.

THE DAY WE MET A BUCKEYE

We were in an Assisted Living Facility right in the middle of the Ohio State Capitol (Columbus).

It was a beautiful Victorian House that had been converted into this facility. We sang a few songs for the folks that afternoon, and then I noticed my wife waving and smiling at someone that was on one of the balconies. So when the song was over, I looked to my left and saw a kind, smiling face of a woman in her wheelchair. She clapped her hands together as not to make any noise and smiled to let us know she was enjoying the music. Then I heard a loud voice from another direction in the room and it was a man sitting front and center. He asked with a robust voice, "Do you know what a Buckeye is?" There he was in his Ohio State robe and slippers, without waiting for my answer; he proudly blurted out, "It's a skinless, hairless, worthless nut! GO '43!!!", obviously a proud graduate. I had then told him one of my brothers had carried a buckeye in his pocket ever since we were kids and that he had been told it brought good luck. Then I told him that I hadn't seen one in a long time and that Leigh Ann had never seen one. He then stood up and said, "I'll be right back, keep on singing." By the time the next song was over, he was back with two buckeyes; one for each of us. We thanked him and let him know that I would carry mine n my pocket and Leigh Ann would carry hers n her purse so every time we sang and played it would remind us of him and all the wonderful people we met that summer afternoon in Buckeye Country.

I wish Woody Hayes, the famous OSU football coach, could have been there the day the Hoosiers met the Buckeyes.

HE SAID "I'LL DO MY BEST"

I had mentioned in a previous chapter that one of our bookings was in a hearing impaired facility. Well one Saturday morning when we were there to sing for them, the woman that usually did the signing was not able to be there. The director thought of John and said that maybe he would help. So she paged him. A facility of that size on a Saturday morning can be quite busy. Often families and friends come to visit, etc...; but John was one of the kindest men I had ever met. He said, "I'll do my best!"

We had all of our equipment set up in the dining room. We also had a copy of the words to the hymns, as well as the special songs my wife would sing with her background music. As we began to sing, I realized John didn't have to look at the words such as "I'll Fly Away", "Joy Unspeakable", "The Old Rugged Cross" and so on. He was singing and signing all of them as if he was working with us every day. Then I noticed as he sang more and more of the *old songs*, he began to turn his face away from us. Then I saw the tears forming in his eyes. I realized while John was trying to help us and those people that day, those *old songs* were bringing back memories of his childhood.

Afterward he told me his mother was the church pianist and how as a young boy he used to sit on the bench beside her and turn the pages. He then shared with me that in his first marriage he had problems and a lot of sadness; but as he began to sing those old songs, he began to remember good things from his life. Things like his mother and Sunday School. How often is it when we reach out to help someone else, we're the ones who get the blessing more than anyone else in the room. He smiled and said, "I was not ble to be in church this past week, but I have een able to be part of this service."

I believe the statements we hear the most are, 'I feel like I have been to church now.", "Why don't you come more often?", "We need more of this.", and "How soon will you be back?" They frequently tell us that they have plenty of food, games, snacks, and outside entertainment. They always tell us of how much more gospel entertainment and scriptures are needed because they cannot get out to church anymore.

<u>So again I challenge you!</u> If you can get involved in a local Assisted Living Facility or Nursing Home ~ **PLEASE DO!**

The missionaries have a saying in their ministry, "If you can't go, then you <u>must</u> send." We encourage you that if for some reason you yourself are not able to go to these places and help these people, send someone from your church ~ get your youth involved. Work with them and encourage them today!!! Back them in every way!! We lose people every week in those facilities, so don't wait. In the words of those Seniors, "Why don't you come more often?! **Please**."

WE NEVER KNOW WHO'S LISTENING

This was our first time to sing, play, and tells this new group of people that God really loves them. All new faces and yet group after group seem to look alike; so many times I just knew I'd seen that same person in another facility, in another state, but we knew this was a group of people we had never seen before.

There was one lady in the Chicago area that said, "Oh, I used to watch you on T.V. every week." That was very nice, but even this building was brand new. As we do at all the facilities, I pulled up front and unloaded all our equipment. When we entered the big glass doors there was a lady at a desk that smiled and welcomed us to their new home; and with that, the director met us and showed us where we would set up all of our equipment. We opened our program first with somewhat of a fast song, then we slowed it down a little to see what kind of sound they would open up to best. There are so many different denominations represented in these facilities that we try to find out what most are comfortable with; some love the old camp meeting songs, others like Bill & Gloria Gaither's style of music, while still others prefer the hymns of old from as far back as the 16th & 17th centuries. They all have their favorites, and we do our best to make this time with them as happy and enjoyable as possible.

So we sang and they all began to relax and sing with us until we had to say, "Well, we'd better get on down the road to our next place." As I was taking our equipment out to the car I passed the lady at the desk again, but this time she asked if she could speak with me for just a moment. Big tears were running down her face while she told me, "I couldn't leave the desk to come in for the music, but those beautiful old songs touched my heart; and I want you to know that I'll be praying for you and your wife as you continue to take this musical ministry of yours to others." When we hear things like this, it makes us aware there may be someone that is listening, and we can't see them.

Most of our old songs come from Hymn Books, which were originally sermons by preachers of that day and time. My wife and I are very aware that these are not our words, but God's words from the scriptures, the Bible says, "his word will not return void...", so that is why the tears, that is why the memories (not because of us).

<u>XENIA ~ ANOTHER OHIO TOWN</u>

We were scheduled to be in a very large Assisted Living Facility one Saturday evening in this Western Ohio town ~ Xenia. The way Xenia is pronounced (which is Zeen~ya) is not the way it looks like it would be to me. If however, you are a native of the town it will be pronounced "Zeenie".

When we arrived that evening there was a man (somewhere in his fifties) telling us, while we were setting up, that it was not Sunday and that we should come back the next day because that is the day to have church. Many people were coming into the large room finding their seat and waiting for the program to begin. One of the first ladies I talked to asked me, "Do you know

he right way to say the name of this town?"
"Oh yes." I replied. A business man from that
area had explained it to me and I continued, "We
are in Xenia." I used the long Z sound, and she
smiled and said, "You're alright, you do know;
so many pronounce it wrong.", so I have my ole'
friend to thank for the crash course in how to
pronounce the "X" correctly.

Xenia is known by the weather people as
having the strongest tornado (a class 5) in the
state some years ago. My friend lost his business
and nearly everything he owned; so that is a little
history of Xenia and the "X" sounds like a "Z",
and that evening the weather was just fine.

We began to sing and play as we always do
when the man I mentioned earlier, who the
residents call "Jimmy", walked up and stood as
straight as he could beside Leigh Ann and began
to sing. The people saw what had happened and
began to say, "Jimmy, Jimmy get down, sit back
in your seat." You could see even though he had
some learning disabilities he loved to sing. We
found out that his mother was in that facility and
that there was no one to take care of little Jimmy.
So he lived there also; but instead of helping

him back to his chair, Leigh Ann moved over to him with her mic and let him sing along with us. Jimmy couldn't carry a tune too good, but he didn't let that stop him from doing his best He became a member of the band that night in Xenia, Ohio. Just maybe when we get to heaven the Lord will allow us to get together with all the people that have sung along with us over the years, and I know little Jimmy will be front and center, as well as in perfect pitch.

CHAPTER EIGHTEEN

BACK HOME AGAIN IN INDIANA

Most of the churches I had pastored were in Indiana, our home state.

While in my office studying my notes for the next service, my phone rang. It was one of the ladies from our congregation. She said, "Pastor, my sister has been in a very bad wreck. I was hoping you could visit her." I replied, "I sure will." When I got to the hospital, her injuries were so bad that the doctors didn't have much hope for her to recover. She would never be able to walk again, or take care of herself, and she was a very independent lady.

In a short time the doctors thought she would do better in a Nursing Home. She soon was transferred. A few weeks went by and I thought I would go visit her again. I had played and sang for the people at that facility years ago when it was new; so when I pulled in the drive and went around the parking spaces, it was like seeing an old friend after years of being gone.

I checked in at the Nurse's Station to get her room number. When I walked in, she smiled a very big smile, and one would have never known how sick she really was, being the strong person that she was. I noticed she had her TV turned to a basketball game. It was the Spring of the year, and what is known to basketball fans as "March Madness" (these are the series of games to determine the National Champions). She talked through her pain and smiled of wonderful memories of the local High School winning the State Basketball Championship in 1966. When you do that in the Hoosier State you have to be a special team. This I think is the state game, so much loved that a movie was made called

"HOOSIER'S". As we talked again she smiled, then I held her small cold hands in mine as I said a short prayer just before I left. It wasn't long and I received another phone call from the same sister, but this time it was to tell me that the sick woman had died. I was asked if I would perform the funeral. I assured her that I would be honored to do so.

It's the day of the service. It was beautiful; the place was packed with friends and family. The music was wonderful. I read the obituary from the News Paper as I always do, then as a thought to help family and friends I would tell more of a human interest story. I began to tell about the last visit I had with her and how we were watching what I called the NAACP Basketball Tournament instead of the NCAA. Well at that instant I saw my wife's eyes bug out and a few other Indiana Basketball fans smile and nudge each other. At that moment in the middle of that beautiful funeral, I realized I had misspoken myself, but went right on without missing a beat.

For some that may not know, I meant to say NCAA (National Collegiate Athletic Association), not NAACP (National Association for the Advancement of Colored People).

When the service was over, I wanted to see if any of those smiling faces would say anything to me about my slip of the tongue. No one came forward, except my loving wife, who looked at me and said, "You meant NCAA didn't you?" Then we both burst out in laughter, and I thought what a kick that dear woman would have had to know that even in her death someone smiled.

MAN IN THE WHEEL CHAIR

One evening we headed out of the fourth facility that day taking our music to yet another group. The Western Sky looked beautiful, but by the time we pulled into town we realized how hungry we were, and stopped to get a bite. We saw that the beautiful sky had been replaced with rolling black clouds. Then the rain that followed had drops about the size of silver dollars; not wanting to get our dress clothes wet and wrinkled, but needing to eat before we sang and played again; we jumped out of the car and ran for the eatery. Once inside I said to my wife, "If the

Indians would have had cars, all they would have to do is wash them instead of having to do their rain dance." It always seems every time we clear and wash the car it rains.

We were booked into an Assisted Living Facility where we had been many times before and it had become one of our favorite places As we drove in, there was a large marquee that advertised those who would be appearing (I remember names from Liberace to Merle Haggard). That large building was to our right but we were going to the left. Oh no, no such fare fare ever welcomed us, but we know our pay day is yet to come. There was a middle aged man in a wheel chair sitting about ¾ of the way to the back of the room. He had been injured some years before and now had to rely on other people to push him and take him everywhere he went There was a woman that always brought him out to our service. I really don't remember how many years had passed since his injury, but she had continued to come each evening after work to be with her boyfriend. They knew time was not on their side as they grew older and realized that they could never marry and have a normal

ife and family. As we would sing and try to
encourage them with the scriptures and lyrics of
each song, she would smile at him with the love
n her eyes that anyone in the room could see.
She told us he loves to come out to the music
room whenever we were there.

She got one of our CDs and said she played
t going to and from work every day. All she
wanted was someone to pat her on the back and
tell her what a good job she was doing (and she
was doing that); however, her pay day like ours
was yet to come. Now through the years that
haves passed since that rainy night, I wonder
about the lady and her boyfriend, the man in the
wheel chair. I remember something else though
about that evening. My wife had sung a song and
then played it after our program was over. She
would begin to take our equipment down, and I
would start my job of rolling everything out to
the car. Leigh Ann always played background
music while we got everything out. Remember
this was our fifth performance that day, as well as
all the setting up and tearing down and traveling.
I was so tired, I didn't think I could take one
more step, but the words of that song she was

playing kept me going. The title of that song is "THE CALL" and the chorus goes like this:

So remind me Lord you called me
Sometimes I may be weary
But if one soul is saved it's worth it all
When I see those teardrops falling
Then remind me of my calling
And may I never run from the call.

CHAPTER NINETEEN

FROM THE ATTIC TO THE PENTHOUSE

I talked in the beginning of the book of how I started to play the guitar in the attic of the Old Coolspring Place. I had mentioned how I took my guitar to church, and although I only played in two keys, I gave it all I had to play for the song service; and I continued to go to the Rest Homes and play. I knew my Pastor was not unaware of my lack of variety for the keys in the songs that were being played. Remember? My range was C nd G. The Pastor was a pretty fair Sax Player, but not one time did he act like he knew my lack of music theory ran that deep.

When I left the church to go into my early days of ministry, I was holding one of my first revivals, which was scheduled for three weeks. So you know how long ago that was because today you <u>might</u> get one Sunday, or just one evening service now days.) Pastor and his wife came, and brought another pastor and his wife to hear me preach. Afterward, he was very kind about my music in those early days, but he was also interested in my pulpit skills. They all said nice things about my efforts.

Over the following fifty years I would see him and his wife ever so often. Years later we were both in Florida. He was filling in for a Pastor and his wife who had gone to a convention out west. When he found out I was only about 100 miles away, he called and asked if I would come over and help him out. Well I jumped at the chance, because it had been so long since we had been on the same platform together. I cleared my calendar, and headed for the Gulf Coast. Sunday morning I played and sang. We had a wonderfu time. As he introduced me to the congregatior with tears in his eyes he said, "This is one of m boys." I guess in his mind he never saw me olde and I guess I didn't notice he had grown olde himself.

The most exciting thing that happened wa after the service. He asked, "Will you go witl me this afternoon to the Assisted Living Facility It's just down the street a few blocks. You car play and sing, and then I'll talk to the peopl there and tell them what we had in church thi week." That had a very familiar ring, for it wa all those years ago that Mr. Mac said, "Son, why don't you go with me next Thursday. You car play and sing, and I'll tell them what we studiec in church this past Sunday."

So I said I wouldn't miss it for all the world Off we went to the Assisted Living Facility When we got there it was beautiful. They leac us to the elevator, just my old Pastor and I. Thi time I didn't take a keyboard, no sound effects just my old guitar like Mr. Mac and I did 5C years before. They pushed the top button or he elevator, and right to the Penthouse we went. What a sight, looking all over for miles and miles you could see water, orange trees, and everything beautiful. What difference from the first Rest Home with the goats in the basement, to all these years later.

When my old Pastor began to speak to the people, he said, "I brought the Chet Atkins of Gospel guitar music with me." When he introduced me that way, I thought I better look around to see who in the world he had with him. Then I smiled, and thought well I have learned a few more keys and cords other than just C and G. What a wonderful time, just my old Pastor and I.

As we walked to the elevator to go back down, maybe that's when I realized, yes, time had taken its toll on both of us. Miles and miles of travel, he loved to tell people, "I have preached in every state including Alaska, and Hawaii and 56 countries of the world!" As I looked at him I thought to myself, "He is old enough to be living here himself." There were still miles to go though, and maybe one more foreign country where he could still deliver his message. So when we got off the elevator I asked, "Pastor, car I ask you to do something for me?" He looked straight at me and said, "Sure, what is it?" I knew how prepared he always was for everything, even a little service like we just had that afternoon. I asked him if I could have his notes from the little service that day, and if he would please autograph them to me. He smiled and took out his per from his pocket and wrote, "I love you in the name of the Lord.", and signed it for me. I stil get those notes out from time to time, and smile when I think of the afternoon Pastor and I went to the Assisted Living Facility together, and how over the years how things had changed, but I had a chance at least for one hour that day to go from the "Attic to the Penthouse".

CHAPTER TWENTY

THE LONGING FOR HOME

A man from Africa said to me "No matter how long a tree trunk stays in the water, it will never become a Crocodile." He was living in America, and he loved this country. He had not seen his family in 7 years. His father died, and he was not able to go to his funeral; but his crocodile story was his way of saying he was homesick.

People that live in Assisted Living and Nursing Home Facilities become very homesick. They explain it in different ways like the African, or

like me; when in the middle of the night I was
missing home and I wrote~

Missing My Friends Tonight

I am missing my friends tonight. Someone said, "When
you are young you do everything you can to get away
from home, and as you grow older you do everything
you can to get back." The friends I miss from home are
not just people, but other friends that haven't changed
their address from the first time I discovered them. For
instance, my Old Lake Michigan, or a place I always
went when things were good or bad they call Beverly
Shores. This ~ a place that brings back memories
of me as a 9 year old boy delivering milk, riding and
bouncing along on the old milk truck, or driving past
the old school house and remembering my days there
during WW II. Oh, all those teachers are gone, and I
have no idea where the kids have moved to after all these
years. Many have died and some I can't even remember
their names; but my old friend is still there ~ the old
school house. When I now drive past the building where
I had my business I wave, if I am by myself say, "Hi
old friend!" Even when I pass the cemetery that holds
the memories of Dad, Mom, Grandparents, etc... that
is an old friend too. Yes, the old ball park, and what

is left of the woods on the edge of town. You see ~ these are all my old friends that I took for granted when I was young. I sure would love to spend one whole day with all of them again and realize with old friends neither of us has aged a day.

I must say that out of all the stories I know and have told, this next story is my favorite:

Many years ago, while watching a little TV on Sunday instead of going to church; I watched a church in Atlanta honoring one of its senior pastors who had been retired many years. He was 92 at that time and I wondered why the church even bothered to ask the old gentleman to preach at that age. After a warm welcome, introduction of this speaker, and the applause quieted down he rose from his high back chair and walked slowly, with great effort, and a sliding gate to the podium.

Without a note, or written paper of any kind, he placed both hands on the pulpit to steady himself and then quietly, and slowly he began to speak. "When I was asked to come here today and talk to you, your pastor asked me to tell you what was the greatest lesson ever learned in my 50 odds years of preaching. I thought about it for a few days, and boiled it down to just one thing that made the most difference in my life and sustained me through all my trials. The one thing that I could always rely on when tears and heartbreak, pain, fear, and sorrow paralyzed me; the only thing that would comfort was this verse:

Jesus loves me this I know,
For the Bible tells me so,
Little ones to Him belong,
They are weak, but He is strong.
Yes, Jesus loves me,
The Bible tells me so.

When he finished, the church was quiet. You actually could hear his footsteps as he shuffled back to his chair. I don't believe I will ever forget it. A pastor once stated, "I always noticed that it was the adults who chose the children's hymn "Jesus Loves Me" (for the children of course) during a hymn sing, and it was the adults who sang the loudest because I could see they knew it best." Here is a new version just for us who have white hair or no hair at all. For us over middle age, (or even those almost there), and all you others, check out this newest version of "Jesus Loves Me". It is quite cute, so read, sing, and enjoy.

Jesus loves me this I know,
Though my hair is white as snow,
Though my sight is growing dim,
Still He bids me trust in Him.

(Chorus)

Yes, Jesus loves me,
Yes, Jesus loves me,
Yes, Jesus loves me,
The Bible tells me so.

Though my steps are oh, so slow,
With my hand in His I'll go,
On through life let come what may,
He'll be there to lead the way.

(Chorus)

Though I am no longer young,
I have much which He's begun,

Let me serve Christ with a smile,
Go with others the extra mile.

(Chorus)

When the nights are dark and long,
In my heart He puts a song,
Telling me in words so clear,
"Have no fear, for I am near."

(Chorus)

When my work on earth is done,
And life's victories have been won,
He will take me home above,
Then I'll understand His love.

(Chorus)

I love Jesus does He know?
Have I ever told Him so?
Jesus loves to hear me say,
That I love Him every day.

(Chorus)

I HEAR THE MUSIC, I HAVE TO GO!

ACKNOWLEDGEMENTS

Once again I came back to the little coffee shop with only 7 small tables and two chairs at each table; and I sat down to the same tiny space facing the front windows. The one leg on the table was still wobbling like the first day I sat down and began writing this book. There were snowy days and sunny afternoons when I sat down to my make believe desk. The smell of fresh baked rolls took me back in time to the Old Coolspring Place where Dad worked his magic as a Baker with out of this world bread and one of my favorites, pie slices (Apple or Cherry) ~ thanks Dad.

I am so thankful for my four brothers and my sister that made up the cast of characters at the old home place. Dad and Mom left us a wonderful legacy.

Our two sons that I love the only way I know, with all my heart.

Grandchildren, Great-Grandchildren, Nephews, Nieces, Cousins, Uncles, and Aunts I hope they know how much I love them all.

My Brother Sam for writing the forward for the
book,
a brother and great friend.

Thanks to the secretaries and office staff at the
San Bernardino Community Church in San
Bernardino, CA. for taking the time to proof
read the manuscript.

A special thanks to my Mother-in-Law Carol.
She is an avid reader and agreed to read my first
rough (and I mean rough)
draft of the book. Her words of
encouragement helped so much in
this project .

And a special thanks to all of you who have
read this book, and
allowed yourself to get involved in the
wonderful world of Nursing Homes and
Assisted Living Facility work. If you will listen
close I know you will hear the music also.

~ Thanks to all ~

ABOUT THE AUTHOR

Born December of 1936 in Michigan City, IN the eldest of 6, Frank began his ministry at an early age (15). This book is an adventure of over 50 years in Senior's Ministry, along with other humorous stories.

Frank Manson Pawlak has pastored seven churches, evangelized in several states, has had two television programs, and two radio broadcasts. He is a song writer and author, as well as a father of two sons, grandfather of two granddaughters, and a great-grandfather of three great-grandsons.

He continues his music ministry with his wife Leigh Ann in the Assisted Living Facilities and Nursing Homes, as well as personal appearances.